2

For Your Information

Reading and Vocabulary Skills

Second Edition

KAREN BLANCHARD   CHRISTINE ROOT

PEARSON
Longman

For Your Information 2, Second Edition

Pearson Education, 10 Bank Street, White Plains, NY 10606

Staff credits: The people who made up the *For Your Information 2* team, representing editorial, production, design, and manufacturing, are: Rhea Banker, Aerin Csigay, Gina DiLillo, Christine Edmonds, Laura Le Dréan, Linda Moser, Edith Pullman, Mykan White, and Pat Wosczyk.
Cover design: MADA Design, Inc.
Text composition: TexTech International Pvt Ltd
Text font: 11/14 New Aster
Illustrator credits: Doug Adams (1, 41, 158); Burmar Technical Corp (85, 176, 186, 201, 202, 203); Yoshi Miyake (51, 52, 68); Jill Wood (33, 63, 86, 123)
Photo credits: p. 3 (top) AP Wide World Photos, (bottom) Yoshikazu Tsuno/AFP/Getty Images; p. 9 Courtesy of Judy Gans; p. 17 AP Wide World Photos; p. 26 Eralp Akkoyunlu; p. 49 William Wegman; p. 63 © Jeffery R. Werner/IncredibleFeatures.com. All rights reserved; p. 73 Reprinted by permission: Tribune Media Services; p. 75 Jeff Stine Photo © 1994; p. 79 Rousseau, Henri. *The Sleeping Gypsy.* 1897. Oil on canvas, 51" x 6'7" (129.5 x 200.7 cm) The Museum of Modern Art, New York. Gift of Mrs. Simon Guggenheim. Photograph © 1995 The Museum of Modern Art, New York; p. 81 (left) AFP/AFP/Getty Images, (right) Helen Atkinson/Reuters/Corbis; p. 86 Courtesy of John Buckingham; p. 95 Bettmann/Corbis; p. 105 Bettmann/Corbis; p. 111 Diane Englund; p. 121 Andre Jenny/Painet Inc.; p. 123 (top) Andreu Dalmau/epa/Corbis, (bottom) The Body Shop; p. 128 Mitch Curren; p. 133 Rick Ridgeway © 1993 Patagonia, Inc.; p. 145 Courtesy of David Root; p. 147 NASA FTCSC; p. 152 Royalty-Free/Corbis; p. 169 Stephen O. Muskie/www.outtakes.com; p. 171 Louie Psihoyas/Corbis; p. 177 Courtesy of Chris Kridler; p. 178 Courtesy of Dave Lewison/www.facethewind.com; p. 187 Owen Franken/Corbis

Text credits: See page xiii

Library of Congress Cataloging-in-Publication Data
Blanchard, Karen Lourie
    For your information 2 / Karen Blanchard and Christine Root.—2nd ed.
        p. cm.
    ISBN 0-13-199182-5 (student book : alk. paper)
    1. English language—Textbooks for foreign speakers.   2. Readers.
I. Root, Christine Baker.   II. Title.
III. Title: For your information two.
PE1128.B586 2006
428.6'4—dc22   2006011193

Printed in the United States of America
13   17

This book is dedicated to
Karen's mother, Betty B. Lourie,
and Christine's father, Stanley A. Baker,
for their love and support.

CONTENTS

Scope and Sequence

UNIT	CHAPTER	READING SELECTION	READING SKILL
1 **TUNE IN TO TECHNOLOGY**	Chapter 1	New Robots on Display	Predicting Scanning for Information
	Chapter 2	Online Shopping Is Big Business	Predicting Reading with a Purpose
	Chapter 3	Florida Family Gets Computer Chips	Reading with a Purpose

abcNEWS Video Excerpt: Robot Care

UNIT	CHAPTER	READING SELECTION	READING SKILL
2 **TRAVEL TALK**	Chapter 1	Sailing Around the World	Scanning for Information
	Chapter 2	A Suitcase Story	Recognizing Time Order
	Chapter 3	Flying High but Feeling Low	Predicting

abcNEWS Video Excerpt: Woman Sails Solo

UNIT	CHAPTER	READING SELECTION	READING SKILL
3 **ANIMALS IN OUR LIVES**	Chapter 1	Can Animals Think?	Thinking About What You Know Making a Chart Identifying the Main Idea of a Paragraph
	Chapter 2	Crazy About Cats, or Just Crazy?	Scanning for Information
	Chapter 3	Call the Medicine Man	Thinking about What You Know

abcNEWS Video Excerpt: Congo the Painting Chimp

UNIT	CHAPTER	READING SELECTION	READING SKILL
4 **SETTING GOALS AND FACING CHALLENGES**	Chapter 1	People with Disabilities Find Challenge on Ski Slopes	Skimming for the Main Idea Scanning for Information
	Chapter 2	Breaking Records	Scanning for Information
	Chapter 3	Sounds of Bali	Recognizing Time Order

abcNEWS Video Excerpt: Mike Utley

VOCABULARY SKILL	APPLICATION SKILL
Understanding Word Parts: The Prefix *un–*	Taking a Survey
	Reading Ads
Understanding Word Parts: The Suffixes *–tion* and *–sion*	Debating an Issue
	Writing a Journal Entry
Understanding Word Parts: The Suffixes *–tion* and *–sion*	
Learning Synonyms	Using a Map
	Gathering Information
Learning Phrasal Verbs	Reading Ads
	Writing a Journal Entry
Learning Antonyms	
Recognizing Irregular Past Tense Understanding Word Parts: The Suffix *–tion*	Taking a Survey
	Reading Statistics
	Debating an Issue
	Writing a Journal Entry
Learning Adjectives with the Suffixes *–ed* and *–ing*	
Understanding Word Parts: The Suffixes *–ous* and *–ious*	
Understanding Word Parts: The Prefix *–dis*	Reading a Poem
	Taking a Survey
Using Comparative and Superlative Adjectives	Using a Map
	Writing a Journal Entry
Understanding Word Parts: The Suffix *–able*	

Scope and Sequence

UNIT	CHAPTER	READING SELECTION	READING SKILL
5 **BRAIN POWER**	Chapter 1	Do You Know Your Right Brain from Your Left Brain?	Skimming for the Main Idea
	Chapter 2	Albert Einstein: The World's Most Famous Scientist	Predicting Scanning for Information
	Chapter 3	How Good Is Your Memory?	Reading with a Purpose Identifying Examples

NEWS Video Excerpt: Memory Pill

UNIT	CHAPTER	READING SELECTION	READING SKILL
6 **COMPANIES THAT CARE**	Chapter 1	The Body Shop: A Success Story	Predicting Scanning for Information
	Chapter 2	The Scoop on Ben & Jerry's	Reading with a Purpose Recognizing Facts and Opinions
	Chapter 3	A New Use for Old Bottles	Thinking about What You Know Skimming for the Main Idea Scanning for Information

NEWS Video Excerpt: Giving Back Big

UNIT	CHAPTER	READING SELECTION	READING SKILL
7 **FOOD FOR THOUGHT**	Chapter 1	Space Muffin Wins Contest	Predicting
	Chapter 2	Chocolate: A Taste of History	Thinking about What You Know Recognizing Time Order
	Chapter 3	Do TV Commercials Affect Eating Habits?	Skimming for the Main Idea Making Inferences Scanning for Information

NEWS Video Excerpt: Sugar and Kids

UNIT	CHAPTER	READING SELECTION	READING SKILL
8 **HOW'S THE WEATHER?**	Chapter 1	Are You SAD?	Skimming for the Main Idea Understanding Cause and Effect
	Chapter 2	Tornado Chaser	Identifying Facts and Opinions
	Chapter 3	Climate and Weather	Taking Notes

NEWS Video Excerpt: Blame the Weatherman

VOCABULARY SKILL	APPLICATION SKILL
Understanding Word Parts: The Suffix –ize	Completing a Questionnaire
	Applying Information
Understanding Word Parts: The Suffixes –ful and –less	Using Logic
	Writing a Journal Entry
Learning Homonyms	
Learning Synonyms and Antonyms	Using Your Imagination
	Using the Internet
Learning Homonyms	Writing a Journal Entry
	Reading Business Cards
Understanding Word Parts: The Prefix re–	
Learning Compound Words	Taking a Survey
Understanding Word Parts: The Suffixes –er and –or	Reading Ads
	Writing a Journal Entry
Learning Compound Words with Over and Under	
Learning Synonyms and Antonyms Learning Compound Words	Using a Map
	Understanding Headlines
Understanding Word Parts: The Suffix –ist	Reading a Chart
	Writing a Journal Entry
Using Superlative Adjectives	

The FYI Approach

Welcome to *For Your Information*, a reading and vocabulary skill-building series for English language learners. The FYI series is based on the premise that students are able to read at a higher level of English than they can produce. An important goal of the texts is to help students move beyond passive reading to become active, thoughtful, and confident readers of English.

This popular series is now in its second edition. The book numbers have changed in the new edition and include the following levels:

For Your Information 1 (Beginning)
For Your Information 2 (High-Beginning)
For Your Information 3 (Intermediate)
For Your Information 4 (High-Intermediate)

Each text in the FYI series is made up of eight thematically-based units containing three chapters, which are built around high-interest reading selections with universal appeal. The levels are tailored to help students increase their vocabulary base and build their reading skills. In addition to comprehension and vocabulary practice activities, reading and vocabulary building skills are presented throughout each chapter. Although FYI is a reading series, students also practice speaking, listening, and writing throughout the texts. In trademark FYI style, the tasks in all books are varied, accessible, and inviting, and they provide opportunities for critical thinking and frequent interaction.

The Second Edition

The second edition of *For Your Information 2* features:

- new and updated reading selections
- designated target vocabulary words for study and practice
- expanded reading-skill-building activities
- vocabulary-building skills and word-attack activities
- a glossary of the target vocabulary words used in the readings
- a companion DVD of ABC News excerpts on related themes, with accompanying activities

Using FYI 2

UNITS

FYI 2 contains eight units, each with three chapters. Every unit begins with Points to Ponder questions and concludes with a Tie It All Together section and a Vocabulary Self-Test.

Points to Ponder

These prereading questions serve to introduce the theme of each unit and activate students' background knowledge before they begin the individual chapters.

CHAPTERS

The basic format for each chapter is as follows:

Before You Read

Each chapter opens with Before You Read, a selection of exercises designed to prime students for successful completion of the chapter. Target vocabulary words are introduced, as are background questions, activities, and prereading skills such as Predicting and Reading with a Purpose.

Reading

Each reading relates to the theme of the unit. For variety, the readings include articles, essays, and interviews, among other genres. Close attention has been paid to the level and length of the readings, which range from 300 to 500 words.

After You Read

Readings are followed by a combination of Comprehension Check questions and activities, along with Vocabulary Practice exercises that give students the opportunity to work with the target words from the reading. Introduction and reinforcement of reading and vocabulary skills also fall throughout this section. Talk It Over questions appear regularly, as do culminating activities that require students to practice real-life skills such as taking surveys, reading newspaper headlines, and reading web pages.

UNIT CONCLUSIONS

Tie It All Together

Each unit concludes with activities that encourage students to think about, distill, and consolidate the information they have absorbed throughout the unit. Among these Tie It All Together activities are discussion questions based on the general theme of the unit, an activity that is "Just for Fun," plus new activities based on an ABC News excerpt related to the unit theme. This section also features the Reader's Journal, an opportunity for students to reflect, in writing, on the ideas in each unit. Space for each response is provided at the end of the book.

Vocabulary Self-Test

Each unit closes with a vocabulary self-test to help students review new words they've learned. Test answers are included at the back of the book, to allow students to check and assess their own answers.

References

The FYI approach is based on the following research and scholarship:

Campbell, Pat. *Teaching Reading to Adults: A Balanced Approach*. Edmonton: Grass Roots Press, 2003.

Drucker, Mary J. "What Reading Teachers Should Know about ESL Learners: Good Teaching Is Teaching for All. These Strategies Will Help English-Language Learners, but They Will Help Typical Learners as Well." *The Reading Teacher*, Vol. 57 (1), September 2003.

Pang, Elizabeth S., and Michael L. Kamil. *Second-Language Issues in Early Literacy and Instruction*. Stanford University: Publication Series No. 1, 2004.

Singhal, Meena. *Teaching Reading to Adult Second Language Learners: Theoretical Foundations, Pedagogical Applications, and Current Issues*. Lowell, MA: The Reading Matrix, 2005.

Text Credits

permission from TIME FOR KIDS magazine; **page 158,** Adapted from "Do TV Ads Affect Eating Habits?" by Neepa Shah, *Time for Kids*, February 26, 2004. Used with permission from TIME FOR KIDS magazine; **page 170,** Questionnaire chart adapted from the dust cover of *Seasons of the Mind* by Dr. Norman Rosenthal, Bantam, 1989. Reprinted with the permission of the author; **page 171,** Sources: *Seasons of the Mind* by Dr. Norman Rosenthal, Bantam, 1989; "Sizing Up Sadness According to Latitude" by B. Bower, *Science News*, Vol. 136, page 198; "Cold Weather Blues," *Ladies Home Journal*, January 1989, page 92; **page 177,** Printed with the permission of Chris Kridler.

Acknowledgments

We acknowledge with gratitude the many family members and friends whose reading, writing, and research added so much to this book. We also thank Eralp Akkoyunlo, Desak Made Suarti Laksmi, and Diane Englund for their generosity of time and spirit in agreeing to be interviewed.

We are very grateful to the following reviewers for their valuable feedback on this text: **Robert Baldwin**, UCLA Ext – American Language Center, Los Angeles, CA; **Susan Blahut**, Spring International Language Center, Littleton, CO; **Adele Camus**, George Mason University, Fairfax, VA; **Marta O. Dmytrenko-Ahrabian,** Wayne State University – English Language Institute, Detroit, MI; **Sally Gearhart**, Santa Rosa Junior College, Santa Rosa, CA; **Carolyn Ho**, Cy-Fair College ESL Department, Cypress, TX; **Krista Jack**, College of the North Atlantic, Doha, Qatar; **Susan Polycarpou**, Spring International Language Center, Littleton, CO; **Nicole Ringuette**, College of the North Atlantic, Doha, Qatar; **John Justin Rizzo**, Queens College CUNY – English Language Institute, Queens, NY; **Nina Rosen**, Santa Rosa Junior College, Santa Rosa, CA; **Laura Shier**, Portland State University/IELP, Portland, OR; **Terri Wells**, ESL Services UT Austin, Austin, TX.

Lastly, we thank Laura Le Dréan, Anne Boynton-Trigg, Debbie Sistino, Mykan White, Gina DiLillo, and Aerin Csigay of the Pearson Longman team for their help, enthusiasm, and attention to detail.

We hope that you and your students enjoy the readings and activities in this text and find them interesting *for your information, too.*

KLB, CBR

About the Authors

Karen Blanchard and Christine Root first met when they were teaching at the University of Pennsylvania. It wasn't long before they began working on their first book, *Ready to Write*. They have continued their successful collaboration, producing more than seventeen popular reading and writing textbooks.

Karen has an M.S.Ed. in English Education from the University of Pennsylvania, and Christine has an M.Ed. in English Education from the University of Massachusetts, Boston. Both authors have over twenty-five years' experience working with English language learners at the university level. Karen has also taught at the American Language Academy at Beaver College, in addition to tutoring students at many levels. Christine has taught in the Harvard ESL program and is a founder, coordinator, and guide in the ESOL tour program at the Museum of Fine Arts, Boston. Karen and Christine continue to enjoy working together to create English language textbooks for students around the world.

TUNE IN TO TECHNOLOGY

Technology is changing our lives in many ways. In this unit, you will read about how new technology is changing everything from medicine to shopping.

Points to Ponder

Think about these questions and discuss them in a small group.

1. Look at the picture above. What is the man doing?

2. What kinds of technology do you use most often?

3. Which of the following do you own: a DVD player, an mp3 player, a computer, a cell phone, an electronic dictionary?

4. Has technology made your life easier or harder? In what ways?

New Robots on Display

Before You Read

A Discuss these questions with a partner.

1. What are some things robots can do? How can robots help humans?
2. What are some things robots can do better than people?

B Study these words from the article. Complete the chart. Write each word next to the correct definition.

advice   artistic   athletic
conversations   emergencies

1.	*conversations*	talks between two or more people
2.		able to play sports well
3.		able to create art well
4.		an opinion about what someone should do
5.		unexpected and dangerous situations

SKILL FOR SUCCESS

Predicting
Before they read, good readers guess what the passage is going to be about. This is called **predicting**. To make predictions, read the title and headings. Also look at the pictures and read the captions (the words under the pictures). Predicting helps you understand what you read more easily because you have ideas about what to expect.

C Make some predictions. Check (✓) the ideas you think are discussed in the article.

☑ 1. what the new robots can do
☐ 2. where robots are made
☐ 3. how to make your own robot
☐ 4. when the first robot was made
☐ 5. kinds of robots
☐ 6. what the robots look like

New Robots on Display

↖ Title

Many New Robots

1 Robots of all types and shapes were on display at the World Expo in Japan. The new robots can do many things. They teach people how to dance, have **conversations**, help people in **emergencies**, and much more.

Artistic and Athletic Robots

2 These new robots can do lots of things. A robot named Cooper is **artistic**. It paints pictures. The Batting Robot is **athletic**. It hits balls with a baseball bat. A robot called Caddy-05 is athletic, too. This robot teaches golf. The Partner Ballroom Dance Robot can dance with humans.

Robots Do Important Work

3 Some of the robots do important jobs. They can help people in many ways. For example, Robot ACM-R5 looks like a snake with a camera on its head. It can walk up stairs and swim underwater. It can go into places that are unsafe for people. It looks for lost people after an earthquake. The golden Kinshachi Robot swims like a fish. It goes

This robot goes into the ocean. It checks the safety of bridges and gets information for fishing.

into the ocean to check the safety of bridges and gather information for fishing. Another robot gives medical **advice** just like a doctor. There is even a robotic brain surgeon[1]. It can remove cancer in the brain that human doctors can't reach.

Are They Humans or Robots? ← Heading

4 Some robots look like humans. They talk like humans. They move like humans. But they are really robots. One of the human-like robots is called Actroid Robot. It looks like a Japanese woman in her twenties. It can have conversations in four languages: Chinese, English, Japanese, and Korean.

This robot can have conversations in different ← Caption *languages at the same time.*

·····················

Made in Japan

5 Most of the new robots were made by Japanese companies. Japan is famous for its interest in robots and technology. The Japan Robot Association thinks that in the near future robots will be part of our everyday lives. The association predicts the market for new robots will reach $1.8 trillion by the year 2010. ■

---

[1] **brain surgeon** – a doctor who cuts open someone's head to fix his or her brain

Comprehension Check

A Read these statements. If a statement is true, write *T* on the line. If it is false, write *F*.

_____F_____ 1. Most of the robots at the World Expo look the same.

_____ 2. Some robots can help people in emergencies.

_____ 3. Some robots look like humans.

_____ 4. All of the robots speak four languages.

_____ 5. Japanese companies made most of the robots.

_____ 6. There will be fewer robots in the future.

 SKILL FOR SUCCESS ✓

Scanning for Information

Scanning is a way to read quickly to find specific information. When you scan, move your eyes quickly across the page until you find the information you are looking for, then stop. Think about how the information you are looking for will appear on the page. For example, if you are looking for a date, scan only for numbers.

B Scan the article to match each robot with the correct description. Work as quickly as possible.

	Robot	Description
__c__ 1.	Partner Ballroom Dance Robot	a. looks for people after earthquakes
_____ 2.	Robot ACM-R5	b. paints pictures
_____ 3.	Caddy-05	c. teaches people how to dance
_____ 4.	Actroid Robot	d. helps doctors in surgery
_____ 5.	Kinshachi Robot	e. goes into the ocean to check the safety of bridges
_____ 6.	Cooper	f. teaches golf
_____ 7.	the robotic brain surgeon	g. has conversations in different languages

A Complete each sentence with the correct word.

advice   artistic   athletic
conversations   emergencies

1. Robots help in _____emergencies_____ like earthquakes.

2. Cooper is an _____ robot. It can paint pictures.

3. The Batting Robot is _____. It hits balls with a baseball bat.

4. One robot can have _____ with people in four languages.

5. There is a robot that gives medical _____ like a doctor.

B Circle the correct answer.

1. If you have a <u>conversation</u> on your cell phone, you ___ _____.
   a. talk to someone on the phone
   b. look for the phone

2. An <u>artistic</u> person would probably _____.
   a. hate to paint pictures
   b. paint pictures well

3. Which is an example of an <u>emergency</u>?
   a. a new car
   b. a car accident

4. An <u>athletic</u> person is good at _____.
   a. playing sports
   b. watching sports on TV

5. Which is an example of good <u>advice</u>?
   a. telling your friend to stop smoking
   b. getting angry when your friend smokes

Understanding Word Parts: The Prefix *un-*

A **prefix** is a letter or group of letters added to the beginning of a word in order to make a new word. Learning prefixes can help you expand your vocabulary.

The prefix *un-* is one of the most common prefixes in English. *Un-* means *not* or *the opposite of*. For example, the word *unsafe* from the article means *not safe*.

C Complete each sentence with the correct word.

uncomfortable	unfriendly	unhappy
unlock	unnecessary	unsafe

1. Robots can go in burning buildings that are _____ for people.

2. The little boy is crying. He looks very _____. Maybe he's afraid of the robot.

3. It's not going to rain today. You don't need to bring your umbrella. It's _____.

4. I don't like _____ people.

5. You need to _____ the car door before you get in.

6. My new shoes were so _____ that I had to take them off.

Talk It Over

Discuss these questions as a class.

1. What do you think robots will be able to do in the future?
2. Would you rather have a human doctor or a robot doctor?
3. In what kinds of emergencies do you think robots are helpful?

Design a Robot

Work in a small group. Imagine you could make your own robot. Discuss the kind of robot you would like. Answer these questions about the robot.

1. What is the name of your robot?
2. What does your robot look like?
3. What can your robot do?

On a separate piece of paper, draw a picture of your robot. Choose a member of your group to show the picture to the rest of the class and describe what your robot can do.

UNIT 1

CHAPTER 2

Online Shopping Is Big Business

Before You Read

A Discuss these questions with a partner.

1. Have you ever bought anything on the Internet? What was it?
2. What are some advantages and disadvantages of shopping online?
3. Which items would you buy online? Check them.

  ☐ a. a book   ☐ f. art   ☐ k. a computer

  ☐ b. a CD or DVD   ☐ g. food   ☐ l. a plane ticket

  ☐ c. flowers   ☐ h. medicine   ☐ m. an animal

  ☐ d. jewelry   ☐ i. a car   ☐ n. a camera

  ☐ e. clothes   ☐ j. a TV   ☐ o. a cell phone

B Study these words from the article. Complete the chart. Write each word next to the correct definition.

appearance   convenient   popular

purchase   reservation

1. _convenient_	useful to you because it makes something easier or saves you time
2. _purchase_	to buy
3. _appearance_	the way a person, animal, or thing looks to others
4. _reservation_	an arrangement you make so that you have a place in a hotel, restaurant, plane, etc.
5. _popular_	liked by a lot of people

C Make some predictions about the article. Think about the title. Look at the picture, and read the caption. Make a list of your predictions.

The article will discuss what people buy online.

_____

_____

Reading with a Purpose

Before you read, it is helpful to have a **purpose,** or reason, for reading. We read for many reasons. For example, sometimes we read to relax. Other times we read to learn something. Having a purpose for reading will keep you involved. To set a purpose, ask yourself questions that you want answered. As you read, look for answers to the questions.

D You are going to read about shopping online. What are three things you hope to learn from the article?

1. _____

2. _____

3. _____

Online Shopping Is Big Business

1   Online shopping is big business these days. Using the Internet, you can buy anything from clothes to cars. You can purchase an airline ticket, make a hotel reservation, buy candy, or send flowers. It is not surprising that more and more people are shopping online every day. Why is online shopping becoming so popular? One of the biggest reasons is that it is convenient. Web shopping is quick and easy. All you need is a computer and a connection to

the Internet. It is easy to compare products and prices. You don't need to leave your house, and you can shop anytime you want.

This woman bought her horse online.

2 Cathy Thibeault is a good example of someone who likes to shop online. Cathy lives in southern France. Her childhood friend, Pam Eubank, lives in Massachusetts. Cathy and Pam are both adults now, but they still like to give each other birthday gifts. It's a lot easier with the help of the Internet. Last year, Cathy bought Pam flowers online. The flowers arrived fresh and beautiful on Pam's birthday. For Cathy's birthday, Pam used the Internet to buy a book for Cathy.

3 The size, as well as the number, of things Cathy buys online is getting bigger. A few months ago, she shopped for and bought a horse online! At first, she was worried about using the Internet to buy something as big as a horse. How would she return it if she didn't like it? Cathy said, "It was an Internet sale, but I asked the seller lots of questions about the horse. He e-mailed me photos of the horse so I could see what it looked like. I was happy with the horse's **appearance**. I wanted to see how the horse moved when it walked, ran, and jumped. So he also sent me a video. I liked what I saw, and I decided to buy it." Soon the horse was safely delivered to her home. "I love my horse," Cathy said. "This is my dream horse."

4 Online shopping is changing the way we buy and sell things. There are more than 20,000 shopping websites selling more than 300 million products online. People spend a lot of money shopping online. Last year, they spent more than $211 billion! Online shopping is big business, and it will only get bigger. So will the items we buy.

Handwritten notes:

Similar meanings
- Purchase
- Buy
- famous
- popular
- Hard
- difficult
- make a reservation
- Book (I want to book a rest)

[Handwritten annotation above "appearance": look's like]

After You Read

Comprehension Check

A Look back at the questions you wrote before you read the article. Did you find any of the answers? Which ones?

B Circle the correct answer.

1. Why do people like to shop online?
   a. Shopping online is difficult.
   b. Online shopping is quick and easy.
   c. People like to leave their house to shop.

2. What do you need in order to shop online?
   a. flowers and candy
   b. a computer and a connection to the Internet
   c. a lot of time and money

3. What did Pam Eubank and Cathy Thibeault buy each other?
   a. airline tickets
   b. animals
   c. birthday gifts

4. What else did Cathy buy online?
   a. a house
   b. a horse
   c. a car

5. How many products are sold online?
   a. more than 20,000
   b. more than 300 million
   c. 211 billion

6. How much money did people spend online last year?
   a. more than $21 billion
   b. more than $211 billion
   c. more than $1 billion

A Circle the correct answer.

1. Cell phones are very small and easy to use. They are _____.

   a. convenient   b. unpopular

2. That website is very _____. All of my friends know about it.

   a. purchase   b. popular

3. You should make a _____ at the hotel before you arrive.

   a. reservation   b. purchase

4. Kathy liked the horse's _____. She liked the way it looked in the photo.

   a. appearance   b. reservation

5. I'm going to _____ a computer online this year.

   a. popular   b. purchase

B Answer these questions. Check (✓) Yes or No.

	Yes	No
1. If a movie star is <u>popular</u>, do a lot of people like her?		
2. Can you change the <u>appearance</u> of a room by painting it a different color?		
3. If it is <u>convenient</u> to e-mail your friends, is it difficult?		
4. If you make a <u>reservation</u> at a restaurant, do you plan to eat there?		
5. If you <u>purchase</u> a book, do you need to pay for it?		

Understanding Word Parts: The Suffixes -tion and -sion
A **suffix** is a letter or letters added to the end of a word in order to make a new word. Suffixes usually indicate the word's part of speech.

When you add **the suffix -tion** or **-sion** to a verb, it becomes a noun. For example, if you add -sion to the verb *discuss*, it becomes the noun *discussion*.

Note: Sometimes the spelling of the verb changes when these suffixes are added.

C Complete the chart with the correct form of each word. Use your dictionary to help you.

Verb	Noun
discuss	1. *discussion*
2.	connection
3.	decision
select	4.
reserve	5.

D Circle the correct answer.

1. I will _____ two rooms at a hotel in Chicago.
   a. reservation   b. reserve

2. This Internet site has a big _____ of books to choose from.
   a. selection   b. select

3. Did you _____ your computer to the Internet?
   a. connection   b. connect

4. I made a _____ to buy a car online.
   a. decision   b. decide

Talk It Over

Discuss these questions as a class.

1. What do you think about buying a horse online? Would you buy something as big or expensive as a horse online?
2. Have you ever bought something unusual online? What was it?

Take a Survey

A survey is a list of questions you ask people in order to find out their opinions and behaviors. Take this survey to learn about online shopping habits.

Ask five people to answer the questions in the chart. Share your survey results with your classmates.

Name	Do you shop online?	What do (or would) you buy online?	What don't (or wouldn't) you buy online?

Work in a small group. Use the information in the website ads to answer the questions that follow.

TECHIE CITY

www.TechieCity.com

We have all TV brands and models, and sizes from 4 to 39 inches.

We beat any price.

Buy online and save money.
Check out our prices on these products:
Combination TV/DVDs/HDTVs/
Plasma TVs/LCD TVs/Flat-panel TVs/
Handheld TVs/DVD players and VCR/DVD combinations

BEST ELECTRONICS

If you want it, we sell it online!

Come to us
for all your electronic needs.
We have the best in cameras,
computers, DVD players, printers,
TVs, and video games.

Limited time offer: Home theater projectors and screens on sale. Feel like you're in a movie theater when you watch your favorite movies and TV shows!

www.bestselects.com

DEALS NOW

Now is the time!

We are the Place!

If you want a bigger, better, brighter TV, we have just what you are looking for.

This weekend only, take advantage of our free shpping offer on all TVs 25 inches and larger.

www.DealsNow.com

1. Kerim wants to get his wife a nice gift. He thinks she would like to have a small TV for the kitchen, so she can watch her favorite shows while she makes dinner. Where should he buy the TV? _____

2. Mano loves movies. He used to go to the movies all the time, but now he has a wife and a baby. He wants to buy a home theater projector and screen. Where should he buy them? _____

3. Leonora and Carlos want to buy a new TV for their living room. The one they have now is small and old. They want to buy a 26-inch TV, and they want to buy it this weekend. Where should they buy it? _____

4. Atsuko is moving into a new apartment and wants to buy a new TV. She plans to buy a flat-panel TV so she can hang it on the wall like a painting. A 25-inch TV would be perfect. Where should she buy it? _____

5. Kim gave his old TV to his daughter. He wants to get a new one for himself. Depending on the price, he might also buy a video game for his son. Where should he buy them? _____

Florida Family Gets Computer Chips

Before You Read

A Discuss these questions with a partner.

1. An ID card is a card with your name, photo, and important information. Do you have an ID card? What kind of information is on it?
2. When do you have to show your ID card?
3. Do you think a person's medical information should be available to others? Why or why not?

B Study these words from the article. Complete the chart. Write each word next to the correct definition.

benefits   permission   privacy
suggested   tiny   worry

1.	the act of allowing someone to do something
2.	to think about something that makes you feel uncomfortable or unhappy
3.	very small
4.	advantages or good results
5.	told someone your idea(s) about what to do
6.	keeping personal information secret

✓ **Reading with a Purpose**

C You are going to read about a new kind of technology. Read the first paragraph of the article. What are three things you hope to learn from the article?

1. _____
2. _____
3. _____

FLORIDA FAMILY GETS COMPUTER CHIPS

A New Way to Keep Personal Information

1 Would you want a card that told all your personal information—your health history, address, phone numbers, and even the food you like? What if that card were a **tiny** computer chip[1], and the chip was put under your skin? Does that sound like science fiction[2]? Well, it's real science. A Florida company called Applied Digital Solutions makes such a thing. It's called the VeriChip.

2 Jeffrey and Leslie Jacobs and their son Derek were the first people in the world to have a VeriChip put in their arms. Each chip is about the size of a piece of rice. The chip has important medical information about the person.

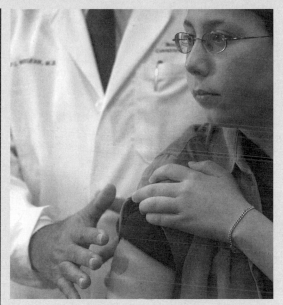

Derek Jacobs, 14, had a VeriChip put into his arm.

3 Derek Jacobs heard about the chip on television and **suggested** that each person in his family get one. Derek's father has cancer, and Derek thought that someday the chip might give doctors important medical information to help other family members stay well. His parents thought it was a great suggestion.

4 This new technology offers many **benefits**. But some people are afraid of how it will be used in the future. One thing they **worry** about is **privacy**. They are afraid that everyone will be forced to get chips. They do not want other people to read information on the chips without **permission**. "The problem is that you always have to think about what the device will be used for tomorrow," said Lee Tien. Tien is a lawyer for a privacy rights group called the Electronic Frontier Foundation.

5 Applied Digital Solutions said it will make sure that the VeriChip is not put in anyone's body without his or her permission. The chips can only be read by special machines called scanners. The company will give the scanners to hospitals and emergency services.

6 Animal owners already use VeriChips to help find and identify their lost pets. Now the company is moving from animals to people. It is working on a new chip that uses satellites[3] to find and identify people who have the chips. These people could then be found anywhere on Earth.

---

[1] **computer chip** – a very small piece of metal or plastic used to hold information, usually in computers

[2] **science fiction** – books and stories about unreal or imagined things in science

[3] **satellites** – objects put in space in order to collect and send information back to Earth

After You Read

Comprehension Check

Read these statements. If a statement is true, write *T* on the line. If it is false, write *F*.

_____ 1. The Jacobses were the first people to have computer chips put in their arms.

_____ 2. The computer chips are about the size of a bag of rice.

_____ 3. Derek Jacobs heard about the VeriChip on television.

_____ 4. Derek thinks the VeriChip will help his father get well.

_____ 5. Everyone likes the idea of putting computer chips in people's arms.

_____ 6. People are already using chips to help find and identify their lost pets.

Vocabulary Practice

A Complete each sentence with the correct word.

benefits	permission	privacy
suggested	tiny	worry

1. The VeriChip is so _____ that it can be put under your skin.

2. Did your teacher give you _____ to leave class early?

3. If you want _____ in your bedroom, you should close the door.

4. Derek _____ that his family get VeriChips.

5. I _____ about my sister's health. She doesn't eat well or exercise.

6. New technology offers many wonderful _____.

B Circle the correct answer.

1. What is a <u>benefit</u> of cell phones?
   a. they are small
   b. they are expensive

2. Which would you need <u>permission</u> to do?

    a. say hello to your friend

    b. use your friend's car

3. When do you have more <u>privacy</u>?

    a. when you live alone

    b. when you share your room with other people

4. Many people <u>worry</u> about _____.

    a. getting sick

    b. taking a walk

5. Which is <u>tiny</u>?

    a. a hospital

    b. a computer chip

6. If you <u>suggest</u> going to a restaurant, you think _____ to go there.

    a. it is a good idea

    b. it is a bad idea

✓ **Understanding Word Parts: The Suffixes *-tion* and *-sion***

C Complete the chart with the correct form of each word. Use your dictionary to help you.

Verb	Noun
1.	information
permit	2.
imagine	3.
4.	identification
suggest	5.
predict	6.

D Circle the correct answer.

1. The VeriChip helps people _____ their pets.
   a. identification   b. identify

2. I like your _____. It's a great idea.
   a. suggestion   b. suggest

3. What kind of _____ is on your school ID card?
   a. information   b. inform

4. I can't _____ a world without computers.
   a. imagination   b. imagine

5. You need _____ to borrow my car.
   a. permission   b. permit

6. I _____ that the price of computers will come down.
   a. prediction   b. predict

Talk It Over

Discuss these questions as a class.

1. Why do you think Derek wanted his whole family to get computer chips?
2. Do you think in the future everyone will have computer chips put into their bodies?

Debate an Issue

Some people think personal ID chips are a good idea. Other people are against them. Which side are you on? Work in a small group. Take turns sharing and explaining your opinions.

Tie It All Together

Discussion

Discuss these questions in a small group.

1. Do you agree or disagree that new technology creates new problems? Think of examples to support your ideas.
2. How do you think technology will change each of these areas?

   - education
   - health care
   - entertainment
   - sports
   - communication

3. Do you agree or disagree with this quotation? Why?

   "The real danger is not that computers will begin to think like men, but that men will begin to think like computers." —Sydney J. Harris

Just for Fun

Find and circle these words relating to technology. The words may be horizontal (→) or vertical (↓). The first word has been found for you.

CELL PHONE
CHIP
COMPUTER
DVD
INTERNET
LAPTOP
MOUSE
ONLINE
ROBOT
SATELLITE
TECHNOLOGY
VIDEO
WEB

```
K T M F Q R O B O T J C K I T Q P J X C
R H D D M S W K D L O C T W H I Z P G E
H Q I K A D Z B V K J J X Z G Z O Z U L
E W M D Q Y B H D Y D L C L N V L K P L
M M W Z K Q P B N Q W Z H A U I W G T P
V W J L B M P P I S F E I P L D I V J H
E G R B O X S H E S Q V P T Z E D B N O
F T E C H N O L O G Y U H O H O P U C N
U U K O R A F Y D Q S Y A P V A M A D E
F W I M M O U S E C E W P P H U H V O C
J D O P P J Q O E D B E K X V B S F E F
Q N L U C H U Z N C O B Q E T A X J B R
W I I T V R F S R D Y J M U Y V A R E Z
H C N E Y J B K L U H O N L I N E L F W
D U U R M I F Q Y I N T E R N E T G V F
H S A T E L L I T E C V S Q V Q Q Z T G
```

Robot Care

In the video you will learn about how robots help doctors in a hospital. What do you think these robots do?

A Study these words and phrases. Then watch the video.

impersonal   in person   operating room

patients   personal touch   surgery

B Read these statements and then watch the video again. If a statement is true, write *T* on the line. If it is false, write *F*.

_____ 1. Dr. Ellison can take care of more patients with the robot.

_____ 2. Dr. Ellison can see and speak to his patients with the robot.

_____ 3. Dr. Ellison's patients like the robot.

_____ 4. Robots can help the doctor in the operating room.

_____ 5. Robots are better than doctors.

C Discuss this question with a partner or in a small group.

What are the advantages and disadvantages of having robots work in a hospital?

At the end of every unit, you will write in the Reader's Journals on pages 205–208. When you write, don't worry about spelling, grammar, or punctuation.

Think about the topics and ideas you have read about and discussed in this unit. Choose a topic and write about it for ten to twenty minutes. Pick a topic from the following list, or choose one of your own.

• your favorite new technology
• robots of the future
• how technology can be dangerous

Vocabulary Self-Test

Complete each sentence with the correct word.

A artistic benefits conversation
emergency suggested worries

1. The family had a long _____ as they ate dinner.

2. My _____ son made me a painting for my birthday.

3. Nooki _____ that we go to the movie before we eat.

4. There are many _____ to exercising.

5. Use this fire exit if there is an _____.

6. My mother _____ about everything.

B advice athletic popular
reservation tiny

1. Did you follow your father's _____ about getting a job?

2. Songs by the Beatles are still very _____.

3. Lukas is _____ and loves to play sports.

4. Did you make a dinner _____ for Saturday night?

5. I can't read the print. It's much too _____.

C appearance convenient permission
privacy purchase

1. You have to ask for _____ if you want to leave class early.

2. She cares a lot about her _____, so she always tries to dress nicely.

3. Doctors must protect the _____ of their patients.

4. We hope to have enough money to _____ a house next year.

5. I think it's more _____ to pay by credit card than by check.

TRAVEL TALK

People travel for many different reasons. Some people travel to visit friends or family. Other people travel for business or education. Still others travel for fun and excitement. As you read the chapters in this unit, think about your own feelings about travel.

Points to Ponder

Answer these questions. Then discuss your answers in a small group.

1. Look at the cartoon above. Do you think it is funny? Why or why not?

2. Why do you usually travel? Check the reasons that are true for you.

   ❑ **a.** for work or business   ❑ **d.** for fun

   ❑ **b.** to visit family or friends ❑ **e.** to relax

   ❑ **c.** for education

3. What do you like most about traveling?

4. What do you like least about traveling?

Sailing Around the World

Before You Read

A Discuss these questions with a partner.

1. Look at the map on pages 202–203. Can you locate these places?

   ⚓Atlantic Ocean⚓   Bermuda   Fiji

   the Galápagos Islands   New York   ⚓Pacific Ocean⚓

   Tahiti   Turkey   ⚓Venezuela ⚓

2. Have you ever been to any of these places? Which ones?
3. Have you ever been on a sailboat? Describe your experience.

B Study these words from the interview. Complete the chart. Write each word next to the correct definition.

adventure ✓   cross ✓   graduated ✓

missed ✓   occasionally ✓   returned ✓

1. *missed*	felt sad that something or someone was not present
2. *adventure*	an exciting experience
3. *graduate*	got a degree
4. *returned*	went back to a place
5. *occasionally*	sometimes, but not often
6. *cross*	to go from one side to another

    Eralp Akkoyunlu is from Turkey. His dream was to build a boat and sail it around the world. Lots of people dream of boats. Many people buy boats. Some people build boats, but very few people build their own boat and sail it around the world alone. Eralp did. Read the interview to learn about Eralp's experiences.

Sailing Around the World

1 **Interviewer:** Tell us a little about your childhood.

Eralp Akkoyunlu: I was born in Turkey in 1933. I spent my childhood on an island near Istanbul called Buyukada, which means *big island* in English. Like many of the children on the island, I loved the water, the fish, and the small sailboats. Sometimes I went out with fishermen on their boats. I was never afraid of the water.

2 **I:** Why did you decide to build a boat?

EA: After I finished my early education in Turkey, I moved to New York to study computer science at Columbia University. When I **graduated** from Columbia, I got a job teaching at Brooklyn College. I loved New York and felt like a true New Yorker, but I often **missed** the sea. One day on vacation in southern Turkey, I realized that what I really wanted to do was build a sailboat and sail around the world. When I **returned** to New York, I started to build the boat.

3 **I:** How long did it take to build the boat? How big is it?

EA: I worked at my teaching job during the week and began to build the boat at night and on weekends. It was a long and difficult job. It took me about five years. The boat is 38 feet (11.5 meters) long. It has two sails and it's made of fiberglass[1]. I decided to name the boat *Yosun*, which means *seaweed*[2].

4 **I:** Describe the trip you took on your boat.

EA: First I sailed from New York to Bermuda. From there, I sailed to Venezuela, then to the Galápagos Islands and Tahiti. I sailed all through the South Pacific Ocean and stopped for a visit on the island of Fiji. **Occasionally**, some friends or family members joined me on the boat. But most of the time, my only friends were dolphins and flying fish. Sometimes a bird would stop by for a free ride or for a little rest. I love the company of the sea, and most of all, I love my boat. *Yosun* sails beautifully and is a joy to see.

5 **I:** What are you doing now? Are you planning another trip?

EA: Now I spend part of my life on the sea and part in the city. *Yosun* is in southern Turkey now. I'm planning a second big trip. I want to **cross** the Atlantic Ocean and then return to the South Pacific. It's going to be a real **adventure**!

[1] **fiberglass** – a lightweight material made from small pieces of glass, used to make racing cars, small boats, etc.

[2] **seaweed** – a plant growing in the ocean

After You Read

Comprehension Check

A Read these statements. If a statement is true, write *T* on the line. If it is false, write *F*.

_____ 1. Eralp grew up in Turkey.

_____ 2. As a child, Eralp was afraid of water.

_____ 3. Eralp studied boat building at Columbia University.

_____ 4. Eralp's dream was to build a boat.

_____ 5. Eralp built *Yosun* in Turkey.

_____ 6. Eralp usually sailed alone.

_____ 7. *Yosun* is made of wood.

_____ 8. Eralp wants to go on another sailing trip.

✓ **Scanning for Information**

B Scan the interview for the answer to each question. Look for key words, numbers, and names to help you find the information. Work as quickly as possible.

1. When was Eralp born? _____

2. Where was he born? _____

3. How long did it take Eralp to build his sailboat? _____

4. How long is the boat? _____

5. What does *Yosun* mean in English? _____

Vocabulary Practice

A Complete each sentence with the correct word.

adventure   cross   graduated
missed   occasionally   returned

1. Eralp loved New York and felt like a true New Yorker, but he often

   _____ the sea.

2. When he _____ to New York, he started to build the boat.

3. _____, friends would join him on the boat, but most often his friends were fish and dolphins.

4. When he _____ from Columbia, he got a job teaching at Brooklyn College.

5. Eralp wants to _____ the Atlantic Ocean and then go back to the South Pacific.

6. Sailing around the world is a real _____!

B Circle the correct answer.

1. Which is an example of an <u>adventure</u>?
   a. a trip to a new place
   b. a day at school

2. If you go sailing <u>occasionally</u>, you go _____.
   a. every day
   b. sometimes

3. You <u>miss</u> people who _____.
   a. are not with you
   b. you see every day

4. Which is the way to <u>cross</u> an ocean?
   a. by foot
   b. by boat

5. What can you <u>graduate</u> from?
   a. high school
   b. an island

6. When would you <u>return</u> home?
   a. before a trip
   b. after a trip

Learning Synonyms

Synonyms are words that have the same meaning. For example, *big* and *large* are synonyms. Learning synonyms can help you expand your vocabulary.

C Read the paragraph. Find a synonym for each word in the chart that follows. Write the synonyms in the chart.

I live in a small town by the ocean. When I was young, I loved to go fishing with the other kids in my town. We felt like real fishermen. One day, we were fishing on a boat and it started to rain. There was thunder and lightning, and we were frightened. It was hard to get back to land. When we finally got home, our parents were very happy to see us. It was a scary experience, but at least we caught lots of fish!

Word	Synonym
afraid	1.
began	2.
children	3.
difficult	4.
sea	5.

Talk It Over

Discuss these questions as a class.

1. If you could go anywhere in the world, where would you go?
2. How would you get there? By plane? Boat? Train? Bus?
3. Would you be interested in sailing around the world? Why or why not?

Write a Travel Magazine

Make a travel magazine as a class. Follow these steps:

1. Choose a place in your native country that you think people would like to visit.
2. Use the Internet or library to find some pictures and interesting facts. Write a description of the place.
3. Put your description and pictures together with those of your classmates.
4. Think of a title for the travel magazine, and have someone in your class design a cover for it.

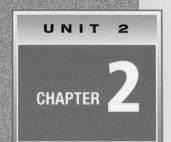

A Suitcase Story

Before You Read

A Answer these questions. Then discuss your answers with a partner.

1. What do you like to do on vacation? Put a 1 in front of the activity you like best, and so on.

_____ go skiing _____ go camping

_____ see sights in a city _____ visit family or friends

_____ go to the beach _____ other: _____

2. How important are each of the following things when you go on vacation? Complete the chart. Check the box that best describes your opinion.

	Very Important	Somewhat Important	Not Important
location			
friendly people			
food			
cost			
weather			
interesting sights			
shopping			
hotel			
scenery (trees, mountains, etc.)			

B Study these words from the e-mail. Complete the chart. Write each word next to the correct definition.

borrow   fortunately   frustrated

mistake   nervous   realized

1.	something you do that is wrong
2.	upset because you can't get or do what you want
3.	worried or frightened about something
4.	understood something
5.	luckily
6.	to use something that belongs to someone else and give it back later

A Suitcase Story

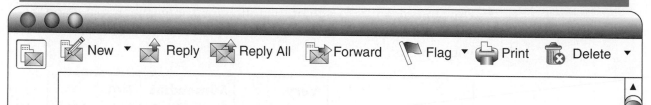

New ▼   Reply   Reply All   Forward   Flag ▼   Print   Delete ▼

From: Connie@buzz.com
To: Angela13@cs.com
Sent: August 17
Subject: a story from Mexico

Dear Angela,

1 Hi! I'm writing to let you know that I made it safely to Mexico City, and I already have a story to tell you.

2 The trip here wasn't easy. The plane was five hours late. It didn't leave until 6:00. By the time I got on the plane, I was very tired, but the flight was so bumpy that I couldn't sleep. The taxi ride to the hotel was no better. The driver couldn't understand my Spanish, so he took me to the wrong hotel. From there, I took another taxi and finally arrived at the right place and checked in. At last, I was happy. The hotel was nice, and my room was perfect.

3   I couldn't wait to change my clothes and eat dinner. But my happiness disappeared as soon as I opened my suitcase. The first thing I saw was a beautiful shawl[1]. I was quite surprised, because it wasn't mine. I looked at the other clothes. They weren't mine either. The clothes belonged to someone else. So did the suitcase. I **realized** that I had picked up the wrong one at the airport. How could I make such a big **mistake**? I was hungry, tired, and **frustrated**. I just wanted to eat and go to sleep. It was cold in my room, but my sweater was in my own suitcase. My eyes went to the shawl in the suitcase. Should I **borrow** it? Would the owner care? I would be very careful with it and put it back in the suitcase before I called the airline in the morning. It seemed like a good plan. Who would know? Who would care? So, I put on the shawl and went to the hotel restaurant to eat.

4   When I got to the restaurant, I took off the shawl and folded it carefully on the back of my chair. I ate dinner, paid the bill, and went back to my room. But I forgot the shawl! I never even thought about it until I was in bed. By then it was too late to call the restaurant. It had already closed. I was so worried about the shawl that I couldn't fall asleep. What if someone had taken it? What if I couldn't find it? It was such a beautiful shawl, and I'm sure it was very expensive. How could I tell the owner that I had taken her shawl and lost it? The more I worried, the more **nervous** I became. At some point, I began to have nightmares[2] about going to jail.

5   **Fortunately** for me, today is a new day. I guess I did sleep a little, because the phone woke me up. The manager was calling me with good news. My waiter had brought the shawl to the front desk. He had my name and room number from the restaurant bill. I think this is what traveling is all about: having a great story to tell. Especially if it has a happy ending.

Love,
Connie

---

[1] **shawl** –

[2] **nightmares** – very frightening dreams

After You Read

A Read these statements. If a statement is true, write *T* on the line. If it is false, write *F*.

People spend six times more money when they visit a new country than they spend when they travel in their own country.

_____ 1. Connie's flight to Mexico was on time.

_____ 2. The taxi driver took her to the wrong hotel.

_____ 3. Connie ate dinner in her room.

_____ 4. Connie took the wrong suitcase from the airport.

_____ 5. The shawl belonged to Connie.

_____ 6. Connie was worried because she lost the shawl.

_____ 7. Connie slept well.

_____ 8. The shawl was returned the next day.

SKILL FOR SUCCESS ✓

Recognizing Time Order
Most stories are written in **time order**. That means the writer tells you what happened first, second, third, and so on. As you read, look for clues that give you information about the order of events. Dates, times, and signal words can help you understand the order of events. Here are some common signal words of time order:

when	before	first	next	last
then	after	second	later	finally

B Number these events so they are in the correct time order.

_____ Connie borrowed a shawl.

_____ Connie took a taxi to the wrong hotel.

___1__ Connie flew to Mexico City.

_____ Connie realized that she had the wrong suitcase.

_____ Connie ate dinner in the hotel restaurant.

_____ The waiter found the shawl.

_____ Connie left the shawl in the restaurant.

_____ Connie took another taxi to the right hotel.

Vocabulary Practice

A Complete each sentence with the correct word.

borrow	fortunately	frustrated
mistake	nervous	realized

1. I feel _____ and afraid when I fly in an airplane.

2. She wants to _____ $5.00 from her sister.

3. Please fix the spelling _____ in the sentence.

4. Greg is _____ because his car stopped working again.

5. When I got to class, I _____ I'd forgotten my book.

6. _____, we got home before the rain began.

B Cross out the word in each group that does not belong.

1. luckily	fortunately	~~honest~~
2. frustrated	happy	upset
3. accident	plan	mistake
4. worried	closed	nervous
5. said	realized	understood

SKILL FOR SUCCESS

Learning Phrasal Verbs

Verbs like *put on* and *take off* are very common in English. They are called phrasal verbs. Phrasal verbs usually have two parts: a verb and a preposition. The meaning of a phrasal verb is different from the meaning of its parts.

C Study these phrasal verbs from the e-mail. Then complete each sentence with the correct verb. Use the correct tense.

check in—to report your arrival at a hotel, airport, etc.

get on—to go onto or in a bus, train, airplane, or boat

put on—to wear or dress yourself in

take off—to remove something

wake up—to stop sleeping

1. We had to _____ at 6:00 A.M. in order to catch an early flight.

2. We _____ the train at noon.

3. Don't _____ your seatbelt until the plane lands.

4. You should _____ a sweater. It's usually cold on the plane.

5. Please _____ for your flight at gate 5.

Talk It Over

Discuss these questions as a class.

1. Have you ever lost your luggage while you were traveling? What happened? What did you do?
2. How do you feel about Connie's borrowing and wearing the shawl? How would you act in this situation?
3. Do you have any travel stories to tell? Share them.

Write a New Ending

Work in a group to make up a different ending to *A Suitcase Story*. Choose someone in your group to tell the new ending of the story to the rest of the class.

Ads and Postcards

A Read these ads for five vacations. Discuss them with a partner. Which vacation would you like to go on?

a.

Ski Vacation in Deer Valley, Utah

COST
$1,700
per person/week

Excellent snow conditions, beautiful scenery, and comfortable accommodations

19 ski lifts
88 trails

ALSO INCLUDES:
Ski school
Rental equipment
Child care
Private lessons
Hotel
Two-meal plan
Ski lift Tickets

b.

Theater Tour of London
One wonderful week!

INCLUDES:

Plane ticket   Bus ticket
Breakfast daily   Hotel
City tour   Theater tickets

COST
$1,800
per person

SEE YOUR TRAVEL AGENT FOR DETAILS.

c.

Two Weeks in Paradise
ENJOY JAMAICA'S BEAUTIFUL BEACHES!

INCLUDES:

COST:
$1,850
per person

* Hotel on beach
* Welcome party
* Breakfast daily
* Tour of the island
* Scuba diving
* Jet skis
* Sailboats
* 18-hole championship golf course

d.

Family Fun Cruise

$1,800
adults
$1,000
children

Magic at sea and on land!

Includes:

Three days on our luxury ship

Three meals daily

Admission tickets to Family Fun World

Entertainment on ship

Activities for children and adults

e.

Outdoor Fun is #1
Go camping in Maine.

Relax and enjoy the beauty of nature.

COST:
$45
per night
per campsite

FACILITIES:
Bathrooms
Barbecue areas

Also Available:
Biking trails
Boat rentals
Fishing gear
Bicycles

B Now read five postcards from people who went on the vacations described in Exercise A. Decide which vacation each person took. Write the letter of the vacation on the line.

Dear Carol,

Hi. This city is wonderful. We go to the theater and see a different play every night. We visited several museums and ate at some delicious restaurants. By the way, I think I'm in love. I met the greatest guy on the tour, and we get along so well. Guess what? He's from Los Angeles, too! I'll tell you all the details when I get back home.

TO: Name
         Address

See you soon,
Andrea

1. Vacation: _____

Dear Beth,

We're having a great time. So far, we've had perfect snow every day, and it's not TOO cold. The kids are taking ski lessons in the mornings and skiing with us in the afternoons. No broken bones yet! Our room is nice, but small. Next year, you and Mike should come with us.

TO: Name
         Address

Take care,
Rachel

2. Vacation: _____

Dear Grandma and Grandpa,

This is the best vacation ever. Family Fun World was great, and now we're back on the ship. There are lots of activities, and we are busy all day. The food is fantastic, and there's so much of it. Mom thinks she gained 10 pounds. We'll be home in two days.

Love,
Miles

TO: Name
Address

3. Vacation: _____

Dear Shelly,

Our first week here has been wonderful! The beaches are beautiful, and our hotel is perfect. Lynn got sunburned the first day, but now she's using lots of sunblock. We've met some nice people, and we usually have dinner with them. We went scuba diving and took a ride on a sailboat. I love it here.

So long,
Gary

TO: Name
Address

4. Vacation: _____

Dear Janet,

This is not my idea of a great time. Greg and the kids love it, but I don't. Now I realize how much I like hotels and hot showers. I'm covered with bug bites, and I hate cooking over a campfire. At least it hasn't rained, and the kids are getting lots of exercise hiking. Only two more days until we can go home and sleep in real beds!

Love, Karen

TO: Name
Address

5. Vacation: _____

Flying High but Feeling Low

Before You Read

A Think about how you feel after a long plane trip. Complete the chart. Check *Yes* or *No*. Then compare answers with a partner.

After a long trip on an airplane . . .	Yes	No
do you feel tired or sick?		
do you feel confused?		
do you have trouble eating or sleeping?		
do you ever get headaches or stomachaches?		
do you continue to feel that way for several days after the flight?		

B Study these words from the article. Complete the chart. Write each word next to the correct definition.

adjust   flexible   healthy
suffer   temporary

1.	to experience pain or sickness
2.	in good physical condition
3.	happening for a short time
4.	to change in order to suit a new situation
5.	able to change easily

C Make some predictions about the article. Think about the title and the headings. Look at the picture. Check the ideas you think are discussed in the article.

- ❏ 1. what jet lag is
- ❏ 2. the best jets to fly on
- ❏ 3. the types of people affected by jet lag
- ❏ 4. when most people fly
- ❏ 5. ways to prevent jet lag
- ❏ 6. the causes of jet lag

Flying High but Feeling Low

What Is Jet Lag?

1 Do you ever feel very tired after a long plane ride? If you do, you could have jet lag. Jet lag is what happens when you take a long plane ride to a place in a different time zone. When you arrive, you might feel very tired and sick for a few days. This is because your body did not **adjust** to the new time yet. You may not be able to sleep at night. You may not be hungry at mealtimes. For example, it might be 8 A.M., but you feel more like going to sleep than eating breakfast. You might also get headaches and stomachaches. Don't worry, though. Jet lag is **temporary**.

What Causes Jet Lag?

2 The main cause of jet lag is crossing time zones. The more time zones you cross, the worse your jet lag will be. The direction you fly is also important. Your jet lag will usually be worse when you fly west to east than when you fly east to west. Since you do not cross time zones when you fly north to south or south to north, you won't get jet lag on those trips.

Who Gets Jet Lag?

3 Jet lag is very common. Over 90 percent of long-distance travelers get jet lag. But some people **suffer** more or less than others. Older people often suffer more than younger people

do. In fact, babies usually do not suffer jet lag at all. **Healthy** people suffer less than people who are sick. **Flexible** people suffer less than people who don't like changes.

How Can You Fight Jet Lag?

4 There are several things you can do to fight jet lag. First, get a good night's sleep before you travel. As soon as you get on the plane, change your watch to the time of the place you are traveling to. During the flight, drink lots of water. But don't drink coffee, tea, soda, or alcohol. You should also move around on the plane as much as possible. When you arrive, spend more time outside than inside. Sunshine helps you adjust to the new time more quickly. ■

After You Read

Comprehension Check

Circle the correct answer.

1. What causes jet lag?
   a. crossing time zones
   b. too much sunshine

2. How do you feel when you have jet lag?
   a. happy and hungry
   b. tired and sick

3. Who suffers more from jet lag?
   a. younger people
   b. older people

Hartsfield Atlanta International Airport is the world's busiest airport. It has an average of 1,250 flights a day and serves more than 80 million passengers a year.

4. What should you do during the flight in order to avoid jet lag?
   a. stay in your seat and drink coffee
   b. drink water and move around

5. When you arrive, what should you do?
   a. stay inside as much as possible
   b. spend time outside

6. Flying in which direction does not cause jet lag?
   a. north to south
   b. east to west

7. Who suffers less from jet lag?

    a. people who don't like changes

    b. people who adjust easily to changes

Vocabulary Practice

A Complete each sentence with the correct word.

adjust	flexible	healthy
suffer	temporary	

1. Mary was sick for two weeks, but now she is _____ again.

2. Jet lag is _____. It usually doesn't last long.

3. People may _____ from stomachaches if they don't eat well.

4. How did you _____ to your new life in the United States?

5. I can get used to changes easily because I am a _____ person.

B Circle the correct answer.

1. What is something you can <u>suffer</u> from?

    a. headaches

    b. good food

2. What is hard for some people to <u>adjust</u> to?

    a. time changes

    b. getting on a plane

3. <u>Flexible</u> people _____.

    a. hate change

    b. aren't upset by change

4. Which is an example of someone who is not <u>healthy</u>?

    a. someone riding an airplane

    b. someone staying in a hospital

5. If you have a <u>temporary</u> job, you will probably work there _____.

    a. for ten years

    b. for a few weeks

Learning Antonyms
Antonyms are words that have opposite meanings. For example, *hot* is the antonym of *cold*. Learning antonyms can help you expand your vocabulary.

C Read the paragraph. Find an antonym for each word in the chart that follows. Write the antonyms in the chart.

Don't worry if you feel very tired after a long flight going north to south or south to north. It's not unusual. And it's not permanent. You may not feel well, but you do not have jet lag. You probably feel tired from the stress of getting ready for the trip. You will feel better after you get some sleep. The symptoms you feel during the flight, such as thirst and motion sickness, are not jet lag either. They are caused by the air pressure in the plane.

Word	Antonym
common	1.
short	2.
sick	3.
temporary	4.
worse	5.

Talk It Over

Discuss these questions as a class.

1. What is the longest plane ride you have taken? Did you experience jet lag after the flight? What were your symptoms?
2. Some people think that eating certain foods helps them avoid jet lag. Do you know of any ways to avoid jet lag?

Make a Poster

Work in a small group. Make a list of travel tips or suggestions. Include at least one tip on how to avoid jet lag. Write your tips on a poster. Choose a member of your group to present the poster to the rest of the class and to explain your tips.

Tie It All Together

Discussion   Discuss these questions in a small group.

1. Do you prefer to travel alone or with a group? Why?
2. Which do you prefer, to return to the places you know and like, or to go to new places?
3. Many people think that traveling helps them understand people from other countries better. Do you agree or disagree with this opinion? Why?
4. Do you like to take pictures when you travel? Do you collect items from the places you visit? What kind of items?

Just for Fun   Write the letters of your first name on the short lines. Then write the name of a country that begins with each letter in your name. Follow the example.

J	Japan
I	Iran
M	Mexico
___	___
___	___
___	___
___	___
___	___
___	___
___	___
___	___
___	___

Are there students in your class from any of the countries you chose?

Woman Sails Solo

This video reports on a woman who sailed around the world alone. What kind of difficulties and challenges do you think she had?

A Study these words and phrases. Then watch the video.

cross the finish line	exhausted	set a record
solo	to be up (all day, all night)	tough
voyage		

B Read these questions and then watch the video again. Circle the correct answer.

1. Ellen MacArthur is in the news because she _____.
   a. set a new record   b. built her own boat   c. made a movie

2. The voyage was _____ days.
   a. 78   b. 28   c. 71

3. Ellen's home country is _____.
   a. France   b. England   c. Africa

4. Sailing around the world was Ellen's _____.
   a. dream   b. job   c. vacation

5. Sailing solo was not _____.
   a. tough   b. exhausting   c. easy

C Discuss these questions with a partner or in a small group.

1. Ellen said, "If you really want to do something, you can." Do you agree or disagree? Can you give an example from your own life?
2. What is something you dream about doing?

Reader's Journal   Think about the topics and ideas you have read about and discussed in this unit. Choose a topic and write about it for ten to twenty minutes. Pick a topic from the following list, or choose one of your own.

- the best or worst trip you have ever taken
- why you like or don't like to travel
- advice for someone traveling to your country

Vocabulary Self-Test

Complete each paragraph with the words from the list above it. Use each word only once.

A adventure   fortunately   temporary

New ▾ Reply Reply All Forward Flag ▾ Print Delete ▾

From: Lynn
To: Julia
Subject: I'm here!

Hi. I made it safely to Beijing, China! My flight was long—
almost 21 hours. When I arrived, I had jet lag. I was very
tired and confused. _____, the jet lag was
1.
_____. I slept really well last night.
2.
Tomorrow I plan to explore Beijing. I know this trip is
going to be a wonderful _____. Write soon.
3.
Love, Lynn

B miss   mistakes   realize

New ▾ Reply Reply All Forward Flag ▾ Print Delete ▾

From: Julia
To: Lynn
Subject: I'm here!

Hi. Thanks for your e-mail. My flight to Brazil took
7 hours. I thought it was a long flight, but now
I _____ that it was short compared to
1.
yours! I'm living with a very nice Brazilian family.
I _____ home a little bit, but I know that's
2.
common. My classes started on Monday. My Portuguese
is improving, but I still make lots of _____.
3.
Write soon and tell me about Beijing!
Love, Julia

C borrowed   cross   frustrated
    graduate   nervous

Dear Kazuo,

I've been in Philadelphia for a week. It's been very different from Tokyo. Every day I walk around the city trying to find out where everything is. Yesterday I _____ a map from my neighbor, but I
1.
got lost anyway. I felt really _____
2.
about that. The streets are very busy here, and sometimes it's really hard to _____ the
3.
street. I'm a little _____ about
4.
starting classes tomorrow. I hope I like them and meet lots of new friends. I can't wait for you to visit me here. Please come as soon as you _____. We'll celebrate here!
5.

                                Love, Keiko

TO: Name
        Address

D adjust   flexible   healthy
    occasionally   return   suffers

Dr. Dana's Health Advice

Question: Dear Dr. Dana, I don't mind changes, and I _____ well to new
1.
situations. But my husband is easily upset by change. He isn't _____ at all.
2.
_____, we fly to Miami to
3.
visit our families. He always _____ from jet lag. For the
4.
first few days, he feels too sick to do anything. He doesn't begin to feel _____ again until it's time
5.
to _____ home. What can
6.
you suggest to help him?

From, Worried Wife

ANIMALS IN OUR LIVES

There are so many kinds of animals in the world that it is impossible to understand and count them all. Scientists have studied, counted, and named over a million types of animals. As you read the chapters in this unit, you will learn more about animals, too.

Points to Ponder

Think about these questions and discuss them in a small group.

1. In your country, is it common for people to keep animals as pets? What animals are popular as pets?

2. Have you ever had a pet? What kind? Did (or do) you consider it a member of your family?

3. Is it the responsibility of people to protect animals? Why or why not?

Can Animals Think?

Before You Read

A Discuss these questions with a partner.

1. What do you think are the most intelligent animals?
2. Have you ever had a pet that was very smart? Describe your pet's behavior.

B Study these words from the article. Complete the chart. Write each word next to the correct definition.

incredible   observed   pretended

recently   spot   tasks

1.	acted as if something was true when you knew it wasn't
2.	jobs
3.	very hard to believe
4.	watched carefully
5.	not very long ago
6.	place

Thinking about What You Know
Before you read, think about what you already know about the topic. You will better understand what you read when you connect the things you already know with the new information in the passage.

C You are going to read an article about animal intelligence. Check the statements you think are true about animals.

- ☐ 1. Animals can make plans.
- ☐ 2. Animals can fall in love.
- ☐ 3. Animals can solve problems.
- ☐ 4. Studying the way animals behave can help us understand more about the way humans behave.
- ☐ 5. Animals have a sense of humor. They can enjoy things that are funny.
- ☐ 6. Animals can learn to communicate with language.

Can Animals Think?

1 Can animals really think? Can they make decisions? For years, scientists have asked these questions. Now, many scientists believe that some animals have the brainpower to understand new situations, make decisions, and plan ahead. The following are just a few of the many examples of animal intelligence that scientists have **observed**.

2 Dandy is a young chimpanzee at the Wisconsin Regional Primate Center. **Recently**, he did something that surprised scientists there. One day, Dandy watched a scientist hide a piece of fruit in the sand. Dandy knew where the fruit was, but when some other chimps came around, Dandy **pretended** he did not know the location.

Later, after the other chimps fell asleep, Dandy went right to the **spot** where the fruit was. He dug it up and ate it. It was **incredible**. Dandy planned ahead and tricked his friends.

3 A heron in Japan also did something surprising. One day she saw some small fish in a pond. She invented a new, creative way to catch them. First, she found a twig[1] and broke

---

[1] **twig** – a very small branch or piece of a tree

it into small pieces. Then, she took one of the pieces to the pond and put it in the water. She even moved it to a place in the pond where the fish would see it. When the fish swam over to the twig, she caught one for her lunch. The heron was able to make and use a tool.

4 Alex is a parrot that lives in a laboratory at the University of Arizona. His trainer, Irene Pepperberg, has been working with Alex for twenty years. She taught Alex to talk, name and count objects, and answer simple questions about them. Alex is very good at these **tasks**. He even says, "I'm sorry" when he makes a mistake. But one day Alex did something that really surprised Dr. Pepperberg. She took Alex to a veterinarian's office for surgery. Alex became upset. When Pepperberg started to leave, Alex said, "Come here. I love you. I'm sorry. I want to go back." Alex thought he was being punished for doing something wrong. He seemed to be able to use language to communicate his thoughts.

5 In Italy, scientists showed how an octopus could learn how to perform a task by watching another octopus do it. One octopus watched another open a jar. The jar had a crab inside for the octopus to eat. After observing how to open the jar, the octopus was able to open the jar himself. Until recently, many scientists thought only mammals[2] could learn by watching others.

6 A gorilla named Timmy had lived alone for most of his life. Then zoo workers brought Timmy to the Bronx Zoo in New York City to live with Pattycake, a female gorilla. Timmy and Pattycake had a baby. After their baby was born, it became sick and the mother and baby were taken away. The zoo workers reported that Timmy became very upset. He wouldn't eat or sleep. He even cried. He looked everywhere to see if Pattycake had returned. It certainly seemed like he had fallen in love.

7 Stories like these raise many questions about animals and the way they think and behave. Today, more scientists believe that animals really can think. ■

---

2 **mammals** – animals, including humans, that drink their mother's milk when young

After You Read

Comprehension Check

A Read these statements. If a statement is true, write *T* on the line. If it is false, write *F*.

_____ 1. Dandy forgot where the fruit was.

_____ 2. Dandy tricked the other chimps.

_____ 3. The heron used a twig to catch a fish.

_____ 4. Alex was happy to be at the vetcrinarian's office.

_____ 5. An octopus in Italy learned how to open a jar.

_____ 6. Timmy was sad when Pattycake left the zoo.

SKILL FOR SUCCESS

Making a Chart
Making a chart is a good way to make sure you understand and remember what you read.

B Complete the chart with facts from the list.

lives at the Bronx Zoo	used a twig as a tool
lives in Wisconsin	learned how to open a jar
fell in love	tricked other animals
lives in Arizona	lives in Japan
can count objects	became a father
eats crabs	likes fruit
eats small fish	used language to communicate
can talk	lives in Italy

Dandy the Chimp	The Heron	Alex the Parrot	Timmy the Gorilla	The Octopus
			lives at the Bronx Zoo	

Identifying the Main Idea of a Paragraph

A **paragraph** is a group of sentences about one topic. The **main idea** of a paragraph is the most important point about the topic. The first, second, or last sentence often tells the main idea. Recognizing the main idea of a paragraph will help you understand and remember what you read.

C Circle the correct answer to complete the main idea of each paragraph.

1. **Paragraph 2:**

   Dandy was able to _____.

   a. plan ahead

   b. eat a piece of fruit

   c. hide a piece of fruit

2. **Paragraph 3:**

   A heron in Japan _____.

   a. likes fish

   b. broke a twig

   c. made and used a tool

3. **Paragraph 4:**

   A parrot named Alex _____.

   a. names and counts objects

   b. uses language to communicate

   c. went to the veterinarian's office

4. **Paragraph 5:**

   An octopus in Italy _____.

   a. ate a crab for lunch

   b. learned by watching another animal

   c. was part of an experiment

5. **Paragraph 6:**

   Timmy the gorilla _____.

   a. fell in love

   b. lived in a zoo

   c. had a baby

F Y I

If intelligence is defined as speed and ability to do tasks, the most intelligent animals, after humans, are chimpanzees, gorillas, and orangutans.

A Circle the letter of the word or phrase that is closest in meaning to the underlined word in each sentence.

1. Dandy pretended he did not know where the fruit was, but he did know.

   a. acted as if   b. was certain   c. was sad

2. Dandy went right to the spot where the fruit was.

   a. place   b. circle   c. letter

3. It was incredible. Dandy planned ahead and tricked his friends.

   a. unbelievable   b. popular   c. common

4. Scientists have observed many examples of animal intelligence.

   a. discussed   b. behaved   c. watched

5. Alex the parrot is very good at the tasks he was taught.

   a. words   b. jobs   c. mistakes

6. Recently, an octopus did something that surprised scientists.

   a. Now   b. A long time ago   c. A short time ago

B Complete each sentence with the correct word.

incredible	observed	pretended
recently	spot	task

1. Have you ever _____ an animal using a tool?

2. I always keep my keys in the same _____ so I won't lose them.

3. It was difficult for the students to complete the _____.

4. We moved here _____, but we have already made lots of friends.

5. My new pet parrot learned to say *hello* in just ten minutes. It was

   _____!

6. The little boy _____ he didn't have any candy, but he really had some in his pocket.

Recognizing Irregular Past Tense

Most verbs in English are regular. Regular verbs add *-ed* to make the **past tense**. English also has many **irregular verbs**. It is important to learn the past tense forms of irregular verbs.

C In the article you read many sentences with past tense verbs. Find and write the past tense form of each of these irregular verbs from the article.

Paragraphs 2–3

1. come _____

2. fall _____

3. dig _____

4. eat _____

5. find _____

6. break _____

7. swim _____

Paragraphs 4–6

8. teach _____

9. become _____

10. think _____

11. have _____

12. bring _____

D Answer these questions in complete sentences. Use the past tense.

1. What did the scientist studying Dandy hide? _____

_____

2. What did the heron in Japan catch? _____

_____

3. What did Dr. Pepperberg teach Alex to do? _____

_____

4. Where did she take Alex? _____

_____

5. Where did zoo workers bring Timmy? _____

_____

✓ **Understanding Word Parts: The Suffix *-tion***

E Complete the chart. Add the suffix *-tion* to each verb to make a noun. Use your dictionary to help you.

Verb	Noun
communicate	1.
invent	2.
locate	3.
observe	4.

F Complete each sentence with the correct word from the chart in Exercise E.

1. The world changed after the _____ of the computer.

2. Some people can really _____ with animals.

3. This map shows the _____ of the zoo.

4. Scientists _____ animals to learn about behavior.

Take a Survey

Ask five people to answer the questions in the chart. Begin each question with, "Do you think animals can...". Share your survey results with your classmates.

Name	. . . fall in love?	. . . use language?	. . . make and use tools?	. . . learn by watching others?

Crazy about Cats, or Just Crazy?

Before You Read

A Discuss these questions with a partner.

1. Do you think cats make good pets? Why or why not?
2. Would you prefer a cat or a dog as a pet? Why?
3. How can pets help people?

B Study these words from the article. Complete the chart. Write each word next to the correct definition.

circumstances   fascinating   greet

indicate   mood   stranger

1.	very interesting
2.	to say hello or welcome someone
3.	to show that something is probably true
4.	the facts or conditions that influence a situation, action, event, etc.
5.	someone you do not know
6.	the way you feel at a specific time

CRAZY ABOUT CATS, OR JUST CRAZY?

1   People who own cats think that they are friendly, **fascinating**, and loving pets. Victoria Voith is a professor of animal behavior at Western University of Health Sciences. She asked 887 cat owners to fill out a questionnaire about their cats. The results of her survey may surprise you.

2   Almost all cat owners think of their cat as a part of the family. In fact, 96 percent said that they consider their pet cat a family member. Many people said that their cat sleeps on their bed, wakes them up in the morning, comes to **greet** them when they come home from work, and acts as a "watch cat" when a **stranger** comes into the house.

3   Birthdays are important for cat owners. About 70 percent said that they give their cat a present for his or her birthday. Would you be surprised if you got an invitation to a birthday party for a cat? A few cat owners (6 percent) give their cat a birthday party.

4   Most cat owners talk to their cats. More than 95 percent said that they speak to the cat at least once a day. About 40 percent said that they talk to their cats the way they talk to children. About 20 percent said they talk to their cats just as they would talk to an adult. And about 35 percent said they talk to their cats as pets. Finally, 13 percent said that they speak to their cats in all these ways, depending on the **circumstances**.

5   Cat owners seem to have a special connection with their pets. More than 70 percent said that they are usually aware of their cats' **mood**. Over half think that their cat is usually aware of their mood.

6   People usually think only dogs do tricks[1]. However, you might be interested to know that 40 percent of the cat owners said that their cats can do some tricks. Popular tricks include fetching[2], making noises, sitting, and rolling over.

7   The results of the questionnaire clearly **indicate** that cat owners feel very close to their cats. Are they crazy about cats, or are they just crazy? What do you think?

[1] **tricks** – actions done to entertain people
[2] **fetching** – going and getting something and bringing it back with you

After You Read

Comprehension Check

A   Read these statements. If a statement is true, write *T* on the line. If it is false, write *F*.

_____ 1. Most people who own a cat think of it as a part of the family.

_____ 2. Birthdays are not usually important for cat owners.

_____ 3. Only a few cat owners talk to their cats.

_____ 4. Some cats are aware of their owner's mood.

_____ 5. Cats are unable to do tricks.

✓ **Scanning for Information**

B Scan the article for the answer to each question. Look for key words, numbers, and names to help you find the information. Work as quickly as possible.

1. Where does Professor Voith work? _____
   _____

2. What percent of cat owners give their cats a birthday party?
   _____

3. What percent of cat owners say their cats can do tricks?
   _____

4. What are the most common cat tricks? _____
   _____

5. What percent of cat owners consider their cats to be members of the family? _____

Vocabulary Practice

A Complete each sentence with the correct word.

circumstances fascinating greets
indicate   mood   strangers

1. My mother was in a very good _____ after she got that phone call.

2. I know her pet died, but I'm not sure of the _____.

3. My dog always _____ me when I come home from work.

4. Most parents tell their children not to talk to _____.

5. Scientific studies _____ that small dogs usually live longer than large ones.

6. It is _____ to hear my parrot talk.

B Ask and answer these questions with a partner.

1. What is the most <u>fascinating</u> thing you have ever seen an animal do?

2. Are you usually in a good <u>mood</u> or a bad <u>mood</u> when you wake up in the morning?

3. How do you <u>greet</u> an older person in your country?

4. Do you usually talk to <u>strangers</u>? Are there any <u>circumstances</u> when you would or wouldn't talk to a <u>stranger</u>?

5. What things do you do to <u>indicate</u> that you care about another person, a pet, etc.?

Learning Adjectives with the Suffixes *-ed* and *-ing*
Many adjectives of emotion and feeling are formed by adding the **suffix *-ed*** or ***-ing*** to a verb. We use adjectives that end in *-ed* to tell how we feel. We use adjectives that end in *-ing* to describe things.

*I was very **bored** during the movie.*   *The movie was very **boring.***

F Y I

The British like pets. Half of all the households in England have a pet, usually a cat or bird.

C Circle the correct forms of the adjectives to complete each sentence.

1. I couldn't understand the directions. They were (confused / ⟨confusing⟩). I was (⟨confused⟩/ confusing).

2. I like this article. It is very (interested / interesting). I am very (interested / interesting) in the topic.

3. I just watched a good movie. The end was (surprised / surprising). I was (surprised / surprising).

4. We had a great time at the soccer game. The game was (excited / exciting). We were (excited / exciting) that our team won.

5. The way animals learn to do tricks is (fascinated / fascinating). I am (fascinated / fascinating) by the tricks my cat does.

Read Statistics

Read the paragraph and complete the chart that follows.

Popular Pets
Americans love pets. A recent survey showed that 63 percent of all American households have at least one pet. Dogs are the most popular pet. Thirty-six percent of American households have dogs for pets. There are 74 million pet dogs in the United States. Cats are also very popular as pets. Thirty-one percent of households have at least one cat. In fact, Americans own 90 million cats as pets. Birds and horses are also common choices for pets: 4.5 percent of the households in the United States have pet birds. That's 17 million pet birds. Finally, 1.7 percent of American households have pet horses. Americans own 5.1 million horses.

Pets	Percent of U.S. Households	Number of Animals
		74 million
Cats		
	4.5%	
		5.1 million

Call the Medicine Man

Before You Read

A Discuss these questions with a partner.

1. What medicines do you use when you are sick?
2. How do you think scientists discover different kinds of medicines?

B Study these words from the article. Complete the chart. Write each word next to the correct definition.

ingredients   mysterious   poison

proud   research

1.	something that can make you sick or kill you if you eat it, breathe it, etc.
2.	strange; difficult to understand
3.	careful study, especially to find out new facts about something
4.	pleased with something you do or have, because you think it is very good
5.	the things you mix together when you are making something

✓ **Thinking about What You Know**

C You are going to read an article about using animals for medical research. Check the statements you think are true about animal research.

❏ 1. We can learn a lot about human health by studying animals.

❏ 2. The ingredients for many medicines come from animals.

❏ 3. It is difficult and dangerous to use animals for research.

❏ 4. Animals should be used for medical research.

Call the Medicine Man

1 One day Terry Fredeking answers his phone. He hears, "We need 10,000 black widow spiders." "No problem," answers Fredeking. Fredeking is an adventurer and a biologist. He goes all over the world looking for animals for medical **research**. In fact, Fredeking has traveled around the world 80 times to find animals that help scientists make new medicines. "If you need it, we can get it," he says.

2 A few days later, Fredeking and his team travel to New Mexico to catch thousands of the deadly[1] black widow spiders. The spiders produce a **poison** that can kill animals, including humans. Scientists want the spider's poison to make medicine. The medicine can help humans who are bitten by a black widow spider. In fact, the **ingredients** for many medicines come from animals such as frogs, snakes, and insects. Fredeking is **proud** that the animals he finds may lead to discoveries that help sick people get well.

3 Fredeking recently traveled to Indonesia to find an unusual animal called a Komodo dragon. Komodo dragons are a kind of large, dangerous lizard[2]. They have harmful bacteria[3] in their mouths. If they bite an animal, the animal gets sick and dies. But if one Komodo dragon is bitten by another Komodo dragon, it does not die. Scientists want to know why. They think the Komodo

Terry Fredeking looks at the animals he caught. The animals will be used for medical research.

....

dragons' bodies have a **mysterious** ability to destroy harmful bacteria in their blood. This protects them. The blood that Fredeking collects could help scientists discover a new medicine.

4 It is not easy to get blood from Komodo dragons. They must be caught alive, but they fight anyone who tries to catch them. Fredeking and his team caught a 250-pound (114-kilogram) dragon. The dragon was very strong. Four men had to hold it down, but it kept fighting. The noise from the fight attracted other dangerous and hungry dragons. "Three dragons ran toward us," says Fredeking. But the men kept the other dragons away with sticks, and Fredeking got the dragon's blood. Then he was ready for his next adventure. ■

---

[1] **deadly** – likely to cause death

[2] **lizard** –

[3] **bacteria** – living things that are so small you cannot see them but that can make you sick

After You Read

Comprehension
Check

Circle the correct answer.

1. The animals Fredeking collects _____.
   a. are used for research
   b. are already dead
   c. are sold as pets

2. Fredeking went to New Mexico to catch _____.
   a. black widow spiders
   b. frogs
   c. Komodo dragons

3. Some ingredients in medicine are _____.
   a. making people sick
   b. deadly to animals
   c. found in animals

4. Fredeking traveled to Indonesia to collect blood from _____.
   a. black widow spiders
   b. Komodo dragons
   c. frogs

5. It is hard to get blood from Komodo dragons because they _____.
   a. are too small to see
   b. don't make noise
   c. are strong and dangerous

6. The Komodo dragons that Fredeking catches must be _____.
   a. sick
   b. dead
   c. alive

7. Scientists want to know why the dragons _____.

    a. are protected from harmful bacteria

    b. grow so big

    c. bite other animals

8. Fredeking is _____ his work.

    a. upset by

    b. proud of

    c. quiet about

Vocabulary Practice

A Complete each sentence with the correct word.

| ingredients | mysterious | poison |
| proud | research | |

1. The main _____ in cake are eggs, sugar, flour, and butter.

2. Scientists do _____ to discover new ways to fight diseases.

3. The child became very sick after she ate the _____.

4. I am _____ of my good grades this term.

5. He has a _____ illness that the doctors cannot understand.

B Circle the correct answer.

1. What would a person be <u>proud</u> of?

    a. graduating from college

    b. listening to music

2. Which is NOT an <u>ingredient</u> in soda?

    a. water

    b. meat

3. If you do <u>research</u> on animals, you _____.

    a. study animals

    b. play with animals

4. <u>Mysterious</u> things are _____.

    a. easy to understand

    b. hard to understand

5. If something has <u>poison</u> in it, you _____.

    a. should not eat it

    b. should eat a lot of it

SKILL FOR SUCCESS ✔

Understanding Word Parts: The Suffixes *-ous* and *-ious*

When you add the **suffix *-ous*** or ***-ious*** to a noun, the noun becomes an adjective. The suffixes *-ous* and *-ious* mean *full of.* For example, if you add *-ous* to the noun *danger,* it becomes *dangerous,* which means *full of danger.*

Note: Sometimes the spelling of the noun changes when these suffixes are added.

C Complete the chart. Add the suffix *-ous* or *-ious* to each noun to make an adjective. Use your dictionary to help you.

Noun	Adjective
fame	1.
humor	2.
mountain	3.
mystery	4.
nerve	5.
poison	6.

D Complete each sentence with the correct adjective from the chart in Exercise C.

1. The story was very _____. I couldn't stop laughing.

2. Everyone recognizes the *Mona Lisa.* It is a very _____ painting.

3. It is important to keep cleaning supplies away from a baby. They are _____.

4. She won't tell us where she's going. She's being very _____ about her plans.

5. That part of Switzerland is _____. Skiing is very popular there.

6. Nathan is very _____. He's going to take an important test this afternoon.

Debate an Issue

Some people think it is all right to use animals for medical research. Other people disagree. Which side are you on? Work in small groups. Take turns sharing and explaining your opinions.

Discuss Proverbs

Proverbs are well-known sayings and expressions. Many English proverbs are about animals. Work in a small group. Match each proverb with the correct explanation. Then discuss what you think each proverb means. Use your dictionary to help you.

Proverb	Explanation
_____ 1. Curiosity killed the cat.	a. You can make a suggestion, but you can't force someone to do something.
_____ 2. When the cat's away, the mice will play.	b. As people become older, it becomes hard for them to change.
_____ 3. The early bird catches the worm.	c. Asking too many questions about something can be dangerous.
_____ 4. You can't teach an old dog new tricks.	d. He acts frightening, but he isn't.
_____ 5. Don't count your chickens before they hatch.	e. Starting early leads to success.
_____ 6. Birds of a feather flock together.	f. Good things don't always happen the way you plan for them to happen.
_____ 7. His bark is worse than his bite.	g. When the person in charge leaves, others behave badly.
_____ 8. You can lead a horse to water, but you can't make it drink.	h. People like to be with others who are similar to them.

Tie It All Together

Discussion

Discuss these questions in a small group.

1. What animals make the best pets? Why?
2. How can animals and humans help each other?
3. What are the advantages and disadvantages of owning a pet?

Just for Fun

Have you ever added and subtracted letters instead of numbers? Consider this example:

— ONE + = ?

The first picture is a picture of a bone, so we print the letters *B-O-N-E*. We are told to subtract *O-N-E* from *B-O-N-E*, so we cross out *O-N-E*, which leaves only the *B*. Next, we must add *E-A-R*. When we do this, we get the word *B-E-A-R*. *Bear* is the answer to the puzzle.

Now try each of the following. Hint: The answer is always a kind of animal.

1. — E + — = _____

2. — Y + — M = _____

3. + — = _____

4. — N + — + — = _____

Congo the Painting Chimp

This video reports on a chimpanzee who makes paintings. What do you think the paintings look like? Do you think they will look different from a painting by a human artist?

A Study these words and phrases. Then watch the video.

auction   canvas   masterpiece
monkey around   the buzz

Famous Artists

Andy Warhol   Matisse   Pollack
Renoir

B Read these statements and then watch the video again. If a statement is true, write *T* on the line. If it is false, write *F*.

_____ 1. Congo's paintings are for sale.

_____ 2. Many people like Congo's art.

_____ 3. Chimpanzees are not really interested in painting.

_____ 4. Chimp art looks like expensive modern art.

C Discuss these questions with a partner or in a small group.

1. What do you think about chimpanzee art?
2. Is chimp art real art? Why or why not?

Reader's Journal

Think about the topics and ideas you have read about and discussed in this unit. Choose a topic and write about it for ten to twenty minutes. Pick a topic from the following list, or choose one of your own.

- a story about a pet you have had
- using animals for medical research
- animal intelligence

Vocabulary Self-Test

Complete each paragraph with the words from the list above it. Use each word only once.

A fascinating   indicate   observed
    pretended   spot   tasks

I think the study of animal intelligence is _____.
1.
Scientists have _____ animals doing many things that
2.
show how smart they are. For example, a parrot named Alex can

perform _____ such as naming and counting objects, and
3.
answering simple questions about them. A chimpanzee named Dandy

_____ he did not know the _____ where a
4.   5.
piece of fruit had been hidden. These observations certainly seem to

_____ that animals are intelligent!
6.

B circumstances   greets   mood
    proud   strangers

I think of my dog as a member of the family. She always

_____ me when I come home, and she seems to be
1.
aware of my _____. She is also very smart. She barks at
2.
_____ but wags her tail at friends. She can look mean or
3.
friendly depending on the _____. I'm _____
4.   5.
of my dog and I think she feels the same about me!

C   incredible   ingredients   mysterious
        poisons   recently   research

The _____ used to make many medicines come from
        1.
nature. Scientists collect and study an _____ number of
                                              2.
plants and animals in order to learn about them and make medicines.
They have _____ discovered certain spiders, frogs, and
              3.
snakes that produce _____ that can kill animals, including
                          4.
humans. Scientists want to do more _____ to find out if
                                          5.
these _____ substances can be used to make new
          6.
medicines.

SETTING GOALS AND FACING CHALLENGES

All of us face challenges of one kind or another in our lives. In this unit, you will read about people who set high goals for themselves and overcame difficult challenges.

Shoe by Jeff McNelly

Points to Ponder

Think about these questions and discuss them in a small group.

1. Do you set goals for yourself? Give some examples.

2. What challenges have you faced when trying to reach one of your goals?

3. Look at the cartoon above. What do you think it means? Do you think it is funny? Why or why not?

People with Disabilities Find Challenge on Ski Slopes

Before You Read

A Discuss these questions with a partner.

1. Have you ever been hurt while you were playing a sport? How? What sport were you playing?
2. Have you ever gone skiing? Do you like to ski?
3. In what ways can skiing be a dangerous sport?

B Study these words from the article. Complete the chart. Write each word next to the correct definition.

achieve   chance   disabilities

equipment   injured   participate

1.	the things that you need for a particular activity
2.	illnesses or conditions that make it difficult for some people to do the things that other people do
3.	to be involved
4.	opportunity
5.	hurt
6.	to succeed in doing something

Skimming for the Main Idea

Skimming is a way to read a passage quickly to find the main idea. When you skim, you do not read every word or stop to look up words you do not know in a dictionary. Look for key, or important, words that give you clues about the topic.

C Skim the article one time. Then choose the statement you think describes the main idea.

1. The resort at Ski Windham serves skiers with disabilities.
2. Special ski programs help people with disabilities reach goals.
3. Skiers with disabilities use special equipment.

People with Disabilities Find Challenge on Ski Slopes

1 Mike Utley can't move his legs. Yet twice a week, he skis down the mountains of Vail, Colorado. Utley was **injured** playing football for the Detroit Lions. He lost the use of his legs and some use of his arms. Today he is in a program at Vail for skiers with **disabilities**. Utley skis using special **equipment**. He sits on a seat with two short, wide skis on the bottom. He keeps his balance with special ski poles. The poles have small skis on the ends. Utley says skiing gives him a chance to go out and live his life. "Football was everything to me," he says. "I began playing when I was seven years old. Now Vail has given me a **chance** to do something else."

2 The program's name is Project Challenge. People with different kinds of disabilities **participate** in the program. Some of the skiers have problems seeing or hearing. Others have lost arms or legs or have hurt their backs.

3 More than 100 of the 520 U.S. ski resorts have programs for people with disabilities. The world's biggest program is at the National Sports Center for the Disabled. It is in Winter Park, Colorado. The Winter Park Center does research and trains instructors. There are many full-time instructors and 1,000 volunteers who are trained to help the

skiers. About 3,000 skiers with disabilities took lessons there last year.

4 The resort at Ski Windham in New York State also has a program for skiers with disabilities. Gwen Allard is the director of the program. She says, "There's a neat place in society for a program like ours." According to Allard, "You see other people **achieve** things they never thought they could do." The program at Ski Windham began as a small program in 1983, and today it is one of the biggest and best in the world. Last year the program gave 2,400 lessons to people with disabilities. As in other programs for disabled skiers, the number of its participants continues to grow. ■

After You Read

Comprehension Check

A Circle the correct answer.

1. Mike Utley was hurt _____.
   a. while he was skiing
   b. during a football game
   c. at the National Sports Center for the Disabled

2. When Utley skis, he uses _____.
   a. special equipment
   b. old skis
   c. a football

3. Project Challenge _____.
   a. teaches people to play football
   b. is for people with disabilities
   c. produces special ski equipment

4. There are programs for disabled people at _____ of the ski resorts in the United States .
   a. all
   b. some
   c. none

5. The Winter Park Center _____.
   a. does research and teaches people with disabilities
   b. is directed by Gwen Allard
   c. is in Vail, Colorado

6. The number of people participating in skiing programs for the disabled is _____.

    a. decreasing

    b. increasing

    c. staying the same

✓ **Scanning for Information**

B Scan the article for the answer to each question. Look for key words, numbers, and names to help you find the information. Work as quickly as possible.

1. How many skiers with disabilities took lessons at the Winter Park Center last year? _____

2. How many volunteers help at the Winter Park Center?

    _____

3. Who is the director of the program for skiers with disabilities at Ski Windham in New York State? _____

4. When did the program at Ski Windham begin? _____

5. How many lessons did Ski Windham give to people with disabilities last year? _____

Vocabulary Practice

A Complete the paragraph with the words from the list. Use each word only once.

achieve	chance	disabilities
equipment	injured	participate

Many of the ski resorts in the United States have special programs for people with _____. Some of the skiers have
                                  1.
_____ their backs. Others have lost an arm or a leg. Still
          2.
others have problems seeing or hearing. The disabled skiers use special _____ to practice their sport. The programs do research,
          3.
give lessons, and give people with disabilities a _____ to
                                                          4.
_____ in something exciting and to _____
          5.   6.
new goals.

B Cross out the word in each group that does not belong.

1. achieve   fail   succeed
2. hurt   injured   helped
3. tools   challenges   equipment
4. activity   disability   injury
5. chance   opportunity   favorite
6. quit   participate   take part

SKILL FOR SUCCESS

Understanding Word Parts: The Prefix *dis-*
The prefix *dis-* changes a word into its opposite. For example, *dishonest* means *not honest.* It is the opposite of *honest.*

C Add the prefix *dis-* to each word. Then write the definition of the word. Use your dictionary to help you.

1. ____*dis*honest   _____*not honest*_____
2. _____approve   _____
3. _____agree   _____
4. _____appear   _____
5. _____advantage   _____

D Circle the correct word or phrase to complete each sentence.

1. He always tells the truth. He is very (honest / dishonest).

2. I think what you are doing is wrong. I (approve / disapprove) of it.

3. We have different ideas about how to solve the problem. We (agree / disagree) about the best solution.

4. I can't find my cat. It (appeared / disappeared) while I was at work.

5. Being tall is (an advantage / a disadvantage) in basketball.

Talk It Over

Discuss these questions as a class.

1. Mike Utley said, "Football was everything to me. I began playing when I was seven years old. Now Vail has given me a chance to do something else." What do you think he meant by this statement?

2. Gwen Allard thinks that there is an important place in society for programs for disabled skiers. Do you agree or disagree with her? Why?

Read a Poem

Langston Hughes (1902–1976) was an African-American author and poet. "Dreams" is one of his best-known poems.

Listen to your teacher read the poem "Dreams." Read it to yourself several times. Then answer the questions that follow. Discuss your answers in a small group.

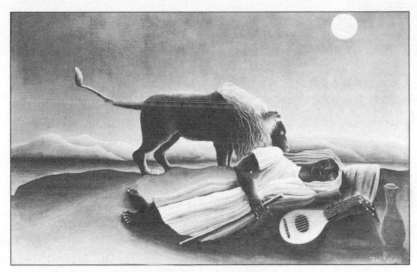

Henri Rousseau. **The Sleeping Gypsy,** *1897.*

Dreams

Hold fast to dreams
For when dreams die
Life is a broken-winged bird
That cannot fly.
Hold fast to dreams
For when dreams go
Life is a barren[1] field
Frozen with snow.
    —Langston Hughes

1. What two images does Langston Hughes use to describe lost dreams?

   _____

2. Why do you think he chose these two images?_____

   _____

3. Why is it important to have dreams and goals? _____

   _____

[1] **barren** – empty

Breaking Records

Before You Read

A Discuss these questions with a partner.

1. Do you like to run or jog? If you do, how often do you run or jog? How far do you go? If you don't, what kinds of exercise do you like?
2. Do you like to run races? To watch them?
3. In a marathon, people run a long distance (26.2 miles, or 42.195 kilometers) to see who is the fastest. Have you ever run, or watched, a marathon? Why do you think people run marathons?

B Study these words from the article. Complete the chart. Write each word or phrase next to the correct definition.

active   compete   reporters

schedule   stay in shape

1.	to try to win
2.	to keep in good health
3.	a plan of what you will do and when you will do it
4.	doing a lot of things
5.	people whose job is to write or tell about events in a newspaper, on TV, or on the radio

BREAKING RECORDS

1   Do you think that younger people are more **active** than older people? Kozo Haraguchi doesn't think so. Haraguchi may be getting old, but he is still breaking records. He set a new world record for the 100-meter race in the 95- to 99-year-old age group. The race took place in 2005 in Miyazaki, Japan. Haraguchi ran the race in just 22.04 seconds. That's fast for anyone. It was his first time running on a rainy day. After the race, Haraguchi told **reporters**, "It was the first time for me to run in the rain and as I was thinking to myself, 'I mustn't fall, I mustn't fall.' I made it across the finish line."

Kozo Haraguchi ran 100 meters in 22.04 seconds.

2   It may have been the first time Haraguchi ran in the rain, but it was not the first time he broke a record. Five years before, in 2000, he broke the record for the 100-meter race for men age 90 to 94. He ran it in only 18.08 seconds.

3   Haraguchi did not start to **compete** in races until he was 65 years old. He said he started running as a way to **stay in shape**. In addition to running, he takes an hour-long walk around his neighborhood every day for exercise.

4   Fauja Singh, age 94, holds a world record, too. He ran a marathon in just 5 hours and 40 minutes. That makes him the fastest marathon runner ever in his age group.

Fauja Singh ran a marathon in 5 hours and 40 minutes.

5   Singh started running only 11 years ago after he moved from India to England to live with his son. Since then he has run five marathons in London, one in Toronto, and one in New York. Recently, he was part of the world's oldest marathon team in Edinburgh.

6   Singh's training **schedule** includes a daily 10-mile walk and run. "I run at least 10 or 12 miles on the weekend, and walk 10 miles every day," he says. He also has a weekly training session with his coach. In addition, he doesn't smoke or drink because he believes it is bad for his health.

7   It seems that Singh gets faster as he gets older. When he was 89 years old, he completed his first marathon in 6 hours and 54 minutes. The next year, he got the same time, which set a world record for 90-year-olds. A year later, he ran even faster, taking 9 minutes off his record time. The following year, he ran the London marathon in 6 hours and 2 minutes. His best time came in the Toronto marathon, where he set a new world record of 5 hours and 40 minutes at the age of 92. That's quite a record for someone his age or any age.

After You Read

A Match each fact with the correct person.

Fact	Person
	a. Kozo Haraguchi
	b. Fauja Singh

_____ 1. was born in India

_____ 2. set a record for the 100-meter race

_____ 3. walks for an hour every day

_____ 4. has a weekly training session with
his coach

_____ 5. started competing in races when he
was 65

_____ 6. ran a marathon in 5 hours and
40 minutes

✓ Scanning for Information

B Scan the article for the answer to each question. Look for key words,
numbers, and names to help you find the information. Work as quickly
as possible.

1. How fast did Kozo Haraguchi run the 100-meter race in 2005?

    _____

2. How fast did Haraguchi run the 100-meter race in 2000?

    _____

3. How many marathons has Fauja Singh run in New York?

    _____

4. How fast did Singh run the London marathon?

    _____

5. How old was Singh when he set a new world record in Toronto?

    _____

F Y I

*Japan has the
highest life
expectancy rate
for both men
(75.9 years)
and women
(81.8 years).*

**Vocabulary
Practice**

A Complete each sentence with the correct word or phrase.

active   compete   reporter
schedule   stay in shape

1. My friend is a _____ for *The New York Times*.

2. My doctor has a very busy _____ this week. I can't get
an appointment with her until next Friday.

3. How many runners are going to _____ in the marathon?

4. My grandfather is old, but he is still very _____.

5. If you want to be healthy and _____, you should exercise and eat well.

B Ask and answer these questions with a partner.

1. What do you do to <u>stay in shape</u>?

2. Do you like to <u>compete</u> in sports events? Why or why not?

3. What is your daily <u>schedule</u>?

4. Would you like to be a <u>reporter</u>? Why or why not?

5. Can older people be as <u>active</u> as younger people?

SKILL FOR SUCCESS

Using Comparative and Superlative Adjectives

Comparative adjectives are used to compare two things that are different. Most one-syllable adjectives add the suffix *-er* to make the comparative form. For example: *old → older*

> *Kozo Haraguchi is **older** than Fauja Singh.*

Adjectives that have more than one syllable usually use the word *more* to make the comparative form. For example: *active → more active*

> *Do you think young people are **more active** than old people?*

Notice these common exceptions:
> good → better
> far   → farther
> bad   → worse

C Write the comparative form of each word.

1. fast → _____*faster*_____

2. difficult → _____

3. expensive → _____

4. dangerous → _____

5. young → _____

Superlative adjectives are used to compare three or more things that are different. Most one-syllable adjectives add the suffix *-est* to make the superlative form. For example: *fast → fastest*

> *Kozo Haraguchi was **the fastest** runner in the race.*

Adjectives that have more than one syllable usually use the phrase *the most* to make the superlative form. For example: *active → the most active*

Austin is **the most active** child in the class.

Notice these common exceptions:

good → the best
far → the farthest
bad → the worst

D Write the superlative form of each word.

1. short → _____*shortest*_____

2. important → _____

3. slow → _____

4. unusual → _____

5. strong → _____

Talk It Over

Discuss these questions as a class.

1. The article begins by asking if you think younger people are more active than older people. Among your family and friends, who is more active, older people or younger people?
2. If you are lucky enough to be alive and healthy when you are in your 80s or 90s, what do you hope your life will be like?

Take a Survey

Find out about your classmates' exercise schedules. Ask four classmates to answer the questions in the chart. Share your survey results in a small group.

Name	Do you have an exercise schedule?	How often do you exercise?	Where do you exercise?

UNIT 4

CHAPTER 3

Sounds of Bali

Before You Read

A Discuss these questions with a partner.

1. Indonesia is a country between Asia and Australia that is made up of 17,000 islands. One of the islands is Bali. Locate Bali on the map below. What do you know about Bali? Have you ever been there?

2. What is your favorite kind of music?
3. Do you play a musical instrument? Which one?
4. Does your country have its own special kind of music or dance? Is music an important part of your culture? In what ways?

B Study these words from the interview. Complete the chart. Write each word or phrase next to the correct definition.

ceremonies   encourage   pay attention
performances   talent

1.	to watch or listen carefully
2.	the ability to do something well
3.	to give someone confidence
4.	presentations of art, music, etc., in front of others
5.	important events that celebrate something

Desak Made Suarti Laksmi is from Bali, Indonesia. She is a famous musician, composer, and dancer. She was one of the first women to play the gamelan, the orchestra of Bali. Read the interview to learn why Desak entered the male world of the gamelan, helping to open the door for other women.

Sounds of Bali

1 **Interviewer:** What can you tell us about the gamelan?

Desak: The gamelan is the most famous kind of Indonesian music. It is the traditional orchestra of Indonesia. There are many kinds of instruments in a gamelan orchestra, such as drums and gongs[1]. A gamelan orchestra usually has at least twenty male musicians. It is very unusual for a woman to play in the gamelan.

2 **I:** When is gamelan music played?

D: Gamelan orchestras play for occasions and **ceremonies** when there is dancing. In Bali, the arts are important in everyone's daily

Desak dances and plays music with an orchestra of Bali.
....

[1] **gong** –

life. We have ceremonies for births, birthdays, marriage, death, and many other events. These ceremonies and festivals always include a lot of singing, dancing, and music.

3 **I:** How would you describe gamelan music?

D: We do not play the gamelan from music that is written down. We learn the songs by ear, according to how they sound. Each musician's part in a song is different. When we play the gamelan, we have to **pay attention** to the sounds everyone else is making. The goal is beautiful, rhythmic sounds. Since all players have to connect to each other to make the music beautiful, we must practice together a lot.

4 **I:** How long have you been playing the gamelan?

D: I've been playing for almost my whole life. My father was a musician and dancer. He played the gamelan. I liked the sounds of the gamelan and began to teach myself to play when I was a very young child. By the time I was ten years old, I was teaching dance and gamelan to children in my family. Sometimes I played with my father.

5 **I:** Did your father **encourage** you to play the gamelan?

D: Oh, yes. He knew playing the gamelan was my dream, and he encouraged me.

Everyone thought that it was unusual to encourage a girl to play the gamelan. But I had a special **talent** for it, so he encouraged me. It was an honor for me to learn to play.

6 **I:** Did you have formal gamelan lessons?

D: Yes, I did. I went to a dance and music high school. After that, I went to the National College of the Arts. When I was there, I began to compose Balinese songs for the gamelan. When I graduated in 1984, I became a teacher at the National College of the Arts. I taught singing, dancing, composing, and gamelan. I have traveled all over Bali teaching gamelan and judging competitions.

7 **I:** What do you do now?

D: My husband and I and our twin sons are now in the United States. We are teaching and giving **performances** on Balinese theater, singing, dancing, and the gamelan.

8 **I:** Are more women learning the gamelan now in Bali because of your success?

D: Well, yes. Now there are some special competitions just for women, and more and more women are playing the gamelan. It's wonderful to see so many female gamelan players.

After You Read

Comprehension Check

A Read these statements. If a statement is true, write *T* on the line. If it is false, write *F*.

_____ 1. In Balinese society, both men and women have always played the gamelan.

_____ 2. Drums are the only instrument in a gamelan orchestra.

_____ 3. The goal of gamelan music is beautiful, rhythmic sounds.

_____ 4. The gamelan is usually played from music that is written down.

_____ 5. The arts are important in the daily lives of the Balinese people.

_____ 6. Music is an important part of many ceremonies and festivals in Bali.

✓ **Recognizing Time Order**

B Number these events in Desak's life so they are in the correct time order.

_____ graduated from the National College of the Arts

_____ taught herself to play the gamelan

_____ came to the United States to teach and give performances

_____ became a teacher at the National College of the Arts

_____ taught dance and the gamelan to children in her family

_____ went to a dance and music high school

Vocabulary Practice

A Complete each sentence with the correct word or phrase.

ceremony   encourages   pay attention
performance   talent

1. Ever since she was a child, she has had a great _____ for singing and dancing.

2. If you want to do well, you need to _____ to what your teacher is saying.

3. We went to a great _____ at the orchestra last night.

4. Look at the pictures of my sister's wedding _____. Doesn't she look beautiful?

5. My mother _____ me to practice the piano every day.

B Ask and answer these questions with a partner.

1. Do you have any special talents? What are they?
2. What did your parents encourage you to do when you were young?
3. What are some important ceremonies in your culture?
4. Have you ever been in a performance? What kind? (dance, music, theater, etc.)
5. In which of your classes do you have to pay the most attention?

Understanding Word Parts: The Suffix -able
When you add **the suffix -able** to a verb it becomes an adjective. For example, *believe* (a verb) becomes *believable* (an adjective).

Note: Sometimes the spelling of the verb changes when this suffix is added.

C Complete the chart. Add the suffix -*able* to each verb to make an adjective. Use your dictionary to help you.

Verb	Adjective
believe	1.
enjoy	2.
love	3.
predict	4.
understand	5.
value	6.

D Ask and answer these questions with a partner.

1. What is the most <u>unbelievable</u> thing you've heard lately?
2. What is the most <u>valuable</u> thing you own?
3. Do you think it would be <u>enjoyable</u> to attend a gamelan performance?

Talk It Over

Discuss these questions as a class.

1. Are there any activities in your culture that are traditionally done only by men? Are there any that are traditionally done only by women? Make a list and compare it with those of your classmates.

Men	Women
_____	_____
_____	_____
_____	_____
_____	_____

2. Are any of these traditional roles changing in your country? For example, are more women doing traditionally male activities today?

Tie It All Together

Discussion

Discuss these questions in a small group.

1. The author Anaïs Nin once said, "Dreams are necessary to life." Based on your own experience, is this true or untrue? Give examples to support your opinion.

2. Jesse Jackson is an African-American religious and civil rights leader. He said, "We've removed the ceiling[1] above our dreams. There are no more impossible dreams." Do you agree or disagree with his statement? Why?

3. Do you think that there are any challenges that are too difficult to face?

[1] **ceiling** – the top surface of a room

Just for Fun

Complete the crossword puzzle. Use the information in this unit and your dictionary or the Internet to help you find the answers.

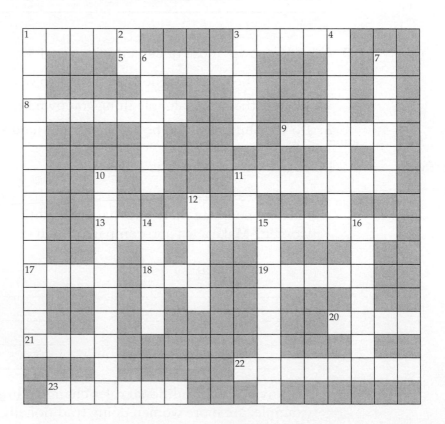

ACROSS	DOWN
1. arms and legs	1. a famous African-American poet
3. backbone	2. abbreviation for *steam ship*
5. where you go to take classes	3. the side of a mountain
8. orchestra in Bali	4. a word that means *to give someone confidence*
9. one of the instruments played in an orchestra or band	6. When you take a risk, you take a ___.
11. small rivers	7. Many resorts have programs for disabled ___.
13. the opposite of *exactly*	10. We all have to face ___.
17. a purpose	11. something you can do in winter
18. Yoko ___ is an artist.	12. It was a great ___ for Desak to learn the gamelan.
19. something skiers and runners participate in	14. a synonym for *evidence*
20. A nickel is a ___.	15. a 26-mile race
21. Many people like to ___ songs.	16. another word for *classes*
22. a person who writes music	
23. home of the first marathon	

Video Activity

Mike Utley

You will see a video about Mike Utley. What do you remember about him from the first article in this unit? What do you think you will see Mike Utley do?

A Study these words and phrases. Then watch the video.

be an advocate for	find a cure	make the most of (something)
paralysis	quadriplegic	take steps

B Read the list of activities. Watch the video again and write each activity in the correct box.

cure every kid   help other disabled people   play football
ski   take a few steps   walk without help

Mike Utley can . . .	Mike Utley can't . . .

C Discuss these questions with a partner or in a small group.

1. What are some adjectives that describe Mike Utley?
2. How does his story make you feel?
3. Do you think he will walk someday?

Reader's Journal   Think about the people and ideas you have read about and discussed in this unit. Choose a topic and write about it for ten to twenty minutes. Pick a topic from the following list, or choose one of your own.

• a challenge you have faced in the past
• someone who has inspired you
• a goal you have set for yourself
• Write your own poem called "Dreams."

Vocabulary Self-Test

Complete each sentence with the correct word or phrase.

A achieve   chance   encouraged
   performance   schedule   talent

1. Van Gogh was a great painter. He had a real _____ for painting.

2. The coach _____ her to try out for the baseball team.

3. I saw a wonderful _____ of the ballet *Swan Lake* when I was in St. Petersburg, Russia.

4. If you try very hard, you can _____ your goals.

5. Pedro applied for a scholarship. He is a good student, and he has a good _____ of winning it.

6. I'm not sure I'll be able to finish the job this week. I have a very full _____ .

B active   compete   equipment
   injured   pay attention

1. Our company is small. We can't _____ with big companies that have more money.

2. You must _____ to the cars around you when you drive.

3. Jacques bought new camera _____ for his trip to Machu Picchu.

4. Marietta fell and _____ her right arm.

5. Children are very _____ . They love to run and play.

C ceremonies   disability   participate
   reporter   stay in shape

1. Jeff and Lindsay like to _____. They exercise every day.

2. I love weddings. The _____ are always so emotional and beautiful.

3. He didn't _____ in the golf tournament this year.

4. It's not easy to be a newspaper _____. You always have to be ready to go where there's a story.

5. Ilse can work even though she has a _____.

BRAIN POWER

The human brain is amazing. It controls everything you do—breathing, eating, sleeping, even reading this book. As you read this unit, you will learn about your own brain and how the human brain works. You will also learn some things about the special brain of Albert Einstein.

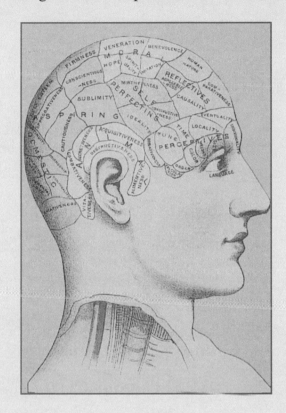

Points to Ponder

Think about these questions and discuss them in a small group.

1. What is (or was) your best subject in school?

2. Do you like to learn new things?

3. What kinds of things are you interested in learning?

4. What interesting things do you know about the human brain?

Do You Know Your Right Brain from Your Left Brain?

Before You Read

A The human brain is divided into a left side and a right side. Take this quiz to see which side of your brain you usually use. Then compare quiz results with a partner.

Are You Right- or Left-Brained?

Circle the answer you most agree with.

1. Which are you better at remembering?
   a. names   **b.** faces

2. Is your desk usually organized or messy?
   a. organized   **b.** messy

3. How do you remember things more easily?
   a. through language   **b.** through pictures

Are You Right- or Left-Brained?

4. When you have to put something together, do you read the directions first?
   a. yes   **b.** no

5. Do you lose things often?
   a. yes   **b.** no

6. When you talk, which do you do?
   a. choose your words carefully   **b.** use your hands a lot

7. Are you more mathematical or artistic?
   a. mathematical   **b.** artistic

8. When going somewhere you have only been a couple of times, do you need to use a map?
   a. yes   **b.** no

9. On what do you base your important decisions?
   a. thoughts   **b.** feelings

10. Do you listen to music while you work?
    a. no   **b.** yes

SCORING: Add up your total number of *a* answers and your total number of *b* answers. If you have more *a* answer, you are probably more left-brained. If you have more *b* answers, you are probably more right-brained. If you have about the same number of *a* and *b* answers, you use both sides of your brain equally.

B Study these words from the article. Complete the chart. Write each word next to the correct definition.

creative   experiment   logical   memorize
specializes   verbal   visual

1.	to try using new ideas, materials, and ways of doing things to find out how well they work
2.	reasonable
3.	relating to seeing or sight
4.	works in a specific area
5.	relating to talking or words
6.	good at thinking of new ideas
7.	to remember words, music, or other information

✔ **Skimming for the Main Idea**

C Skim the article to answer each question.

1. Which paragraph describes the left brain? _____

2. Which paragraph explains that the human brain is divided into two sides? _____

3. Which paragraph discusses the kinds of people who are usually left-brained or right-brained? _____

4. Which paragraph describes the right brain? _____

Do You Know Your Right Brain from Your Left Brain?

1   The human brain is divided into two sides, or hemispheres, called the right brain and the left brain. The two hemispheres work together, but each one **specializes** in certain ways of thinking. Each side has its own way of using information to help us think, understand, and learn.

2   The left side of the brain controls language. You use this side of your brain when you speak, read, and write. Your left brain is more **verbal** and **logical**. It names things and puts them into groups. It uses rules and likes ideas to make sense and be clear and orderly. You use this side of the brain when you **memorize** spelling and grammar rules or when you do a math problem.

3   The right side of the brain is more **visual** and **creative**. It specializes in using information it receives from the things you see, hear, smell, touch, and taste. This side of the brain likes to dream and **experiment** with new things. It controls your feelings about music, color, and art. You use this side when you draw a picture or listen to music.

4   Although we all use both sides of our brains, one side is usually stronger. Some people are more "left-brained," and others are more "right-brained." Our stronger side influences the kinds of jobs we choose and the interests we have. Politicians, artists, architects, and musicians depend on their right brains. Accountants, engineers, doctors, and lawyers usually rely on their left brains. ■

After You Read

Comprehension Check

A   Check the topics discussed in the article.

❑ 1. the side of the brain that is more logical

❑ 2. the size and weight of the human brain

❑ 3. the side of the brain that is more creative

❑ 4. the types of people that are usually right-brained or left-brained

❑ 5. the part of the brain that controls the heart and lungs

❑ 6. diseases of the brain

B Read these statements. If a statement is true, write *T* on the line. If it is false, write *F*.

_____ 1. The human brain has two sides.

_____ 2. Everyone is more right-brained than left-brained.

_____ 3. The right side of the brain is more creative.

_____ 4. When you solve a math problem, you use your left brain.

_____ 5. Both sides of the brain specialize in the same things.

_____ 6. Artists use their right brain more than mathematicians do.

_____ 7. When you paint a picture, you use your left brain.

Vocabulary Practice

A Complete each sentence with the correct word.

creative   experiment   logical   memorize
specializes   verbal   visual

1. The right side of the brain _____ in using information from the five senses.

2. It is difficult to _____ all the irregular past verbs in English.

3. _____ people have good language skills.

4. The lawyer gave a _____ argument. It made sense.

5. Someone who uses new and original ideas to solve a problem is _____.

6. Some birds can see very well. They have excellent _____ ability.

7. Our teacher likes to _____ with new ways of teaching.

B Circle the correct answer.

1. A person with good <u>verbal</u> skills would probably _____ .

   a. explain something in words

   b. draw a picture to explain something

2. What part of your body <u>specializes</u> in hearing?

   a. your ears

   b. your nose

3. Which is an example of <u>visual</u> art?

   a. painting

   b. music

4. If you <u>memorize</u> the words to a song, you _____ .

   a. can't understand them

   b. know and remember them

5. It is more <u>logical</u> to expect rain when it is _____ outside.

   a. sunny and clear

   b. dark and cloudy

6. <u>Creative</u> people are often _____ .

   a. artistic

   b. athletic

7. If you <u>experiment</u> with the dish you are making for dinner, you _____ .

   a. make it the usual way

   b. make it in a new way

Understanding Word Parts: The Suffix -ize

When you add **the suffix -ize** to a noun or an adjective, it becomes a verb. For example, if you add -ize to the adjective *special,* it becomes the verb *specialize.*

Note: Sometimes the spelling of the verb changes when this suffix is added.

C Complete the chart. Add the suffix -ize to each noun or adjective to make a verb. Use your dictionary to help you.

Noun or Adjective	Verb
apology	1.
memory	2.
real	3.
special	4.
verbal	5.
visual	6.

D Complete each sentence with the correct word from the chart in Exercise C.

1. I think it's difficult to _____ new vocabulary words.

2. Did you _____ to your friend for being late?

3. She wants to become a doctor and _____ in brain surgery.

4. He didn't bring his sunglasses. He didn't _____ it was so sunny outside.

5. Can you _____ the way your childhood bedroom looked?

6. It was difficult for him to explain why he was sad. He couldn't _____ it.

Read these descriptions. Circle *right-brained* or *left-brained* to complete the statement at the end of each item. Then discuss your choices in a small group.

1. Daniel DuVal's interest is drawing cartoons. He loves surprises and hates following a schedule. He is very sensitive and likes to find new ways of doing things.

   Daniel is probably (right-brained / left-brained).

2. Dr. Curley is careful about keeping his appointments. He is always on time and does things in an orderly way. Every day, before he goes to work, he goes jogging for a half hour.

   Dr. Curley is probably (right-brained / left-brained).

3. Debbie Gomez is a successful lawyer in New York. Her language skills are very good. She is a very logical person. She gets up, eats, and goes to sleep at the same time every day.

   Debbie is probably (right-brained / left-brained).

4. Ian Baker is the mayor of a small city. He is always looking for creative ways to solve the city's problems. In his spare time, he enjoys going to concerts and playing the piano.

   Ian is probably (right-brained / left-brained).

Albert Einstein: The World's Most Famous Scientist

Before You Read

A Discuss these questions with a partner.

1. What famous scientists have you heard of?
2. What do you know about Albert Einstein?
3. Would you like to study time and energy? Why or why not?

B Study these words from the article. Complete the chart. Write each word next to the correct definition.

curious   genius   immigrated
revolutionized   shy   suddenly

1.	uncomfortable meeting and speaking with other people
2.	an extremely intelligent person
3.	wanting to know about or learn new things
4.	quickly and without being expected
5.	completely changed the way people think or do things
6.	came to live in a new country

✓**Predicting**

C Make some predictions about the article. Think about the title and headings. Look at the picture, and read the caption. Make a list of your predictions.

_____

_____

_____

Albert Einstein: The World's Most Famous Scientist

A Curious Child

1   Albert Einstein was born in Germany in 1879. As a child, he was very **shy** and quiet. He did not talk at all until age three. According to one story, young Albert **suddenly** spoke at the dinner table one night. He said, "The soup is too hot." His parents asked, "Why haven't you ever said a word until now?" Albert replied, "Because up to now everything was all right."

2   Albert may have been quiet, but he was always thoughtful and very **curious**. His limitless curiosity showed up in the questions he asked. For example, at age five he asked, "Why does a compass[1] needle always point in the same direction?" When he was fourteen he asked, "What would the world look like if I rode on a beam[2] of light?" He never lost his curiosity. As an adult he said, "The important thing is to not stop questioning."

*Albert Einstein (1879–1955) is considered a **genius**. His ideas changed the way we think about the unIverse.*

Revolutionizing Science

3   In 1905, Einstein wrote four important papers. The ideas he wrote about **revolutionized** the ways people thought about space and time. In 1915, he published his theory of relativity. His famous equation, $E = mc^2$, explains the relationship between energy and time. It became one of the most important laws of physics. He won the Nobel Prize for physics in 1921.

---

[1] **compass** – an instrument that shows directions
[2] **beam** – a line of light from a bright object

Life in the United States

4 Einstein **immigrated** to the United States in 1933 and became a United States citizen in 1940. Einstein joined the Institute for Advanced Studies in Princeton, New Jersey. He lived a quiet life. He enjoyed classical music and played the violin. One day, after Einstein played with a group of musicians, one of them said, "He'd be a good musician if only he could count!" This was a funny thing to say about Einstein, because his life's work involved very complicated math.

5 Einstein kept his sense of humor throughout his life. A magazine called *Scientific American* once had a competition for the best short explanation of the theory of relativity. Einstein said, "I'm the only one of my friends who is not entering. I don't believe I could do it."

6 Albert Einstein died on April 18, 1955, in Princeton, New Jersey. He had changed the world. In 1999, *Time* magazine named him the "Person of the Century."

After You Read

Comprehension Check

A Read these statements. If a statement is true, write *T* on the line. If it is false, write *F.*

_____ 1. Albert Einstein learned to talk at a very early age.

_____ 2. Einstein was curious throughout his whole life.

_____ 3. His theory of relativity changed physics.

_____ 4. Einstein lived in Germany his entire life.

_____ 5. Einstein had a good sense of humor.

_____ 6. He had a very active social life.

_____ 7. One of Einstein's interests was playing the violin.

_____ 8. Einstein won the Nobel Prize for physics.

B Scan the article for the answer to each question. Look for key words, numbers, and names to help you find the information. Work as quickly as possible.

1. Where was Einstein born? _____

2. When did he publish his papers about the theory of relativity? _____

3. What prize did he win in 1921? _____

4. What was his famous equation? _____

5. When did he become an American citizen? _____

6. When did *Time* magazine name Einstein "Person of the Century"? _____

7. When did he die? _____

Vocabulary Practice

A Complete each sentence with the correct word.

curious	genius	immigrated
revolutionized	shy	suddenly

1. The invention of the automobile _____ the way we live.

2. We had to stop our tennis game when it _____ began to rain.

3. Einstein _____ to the United States in 1933.

4. Einstein was a mathematical _____ .

5. Children are often more _____ than adults They want to know everything about the world around them.

6. He is too _____ to talk in class.

B Cross out the word in each group that does not belong.

1. bored   curious   interested
2. immigrated   moved   listened
3. organized   changed   revolutionized
4. suddenly   quickly   slowly
5. shy   quiet   logical

Understanding Word Parts: The Suffixes -*ful* and -*less*
The suffix -*ful* means *full of.* For example, when you add -*ful* to the word *meaning*, it becomes *meaningful*, which means *full of meaning.*

The suffix -*less* means *without.* When you add the suffix -*less* to the word *meaning*, it becomes *meaningless*, which means *without meaning.*

C Complete these sentences. Add the correct suffix (-*ful* or -*less*) to the word listed.

1. **use**

    a. I can use the information I learned in this class. It is
    _____*useful*_____ information.

    b. I can't use this information. It is _____.

2. **care**

    a. She painted the room with great care. She is a _____ painter.

    b. He didn't pay any attention when he painted. He was
    _____.

3. **help**

    a. Babies need help and protection. They are _____.

    b. My teacher helps me when I don't understand something. She is
    very _____.

4. **pain**

    a. I went to the dentist. I cried when he pulled my tooth because it
    was so _____.

    b. I went to the dentist. He gave me some medicine before he pulled
    my tooth. It was _____.

5. **fear**

    a. He has no fear of dangerous things. He is _____.

    b. She is afraid she'll get sick. She is _____ of getting
    the disease.

Discuss these questions as a class.

1. Read the following quotations by Albert Einstein. What do you think they mean?
   - "Imagination is more important than knowledge."
   - "Do not worry about your difficulties in mathematics. I can assure you that mine are still greater."
   - "It is a miracle that curiosity survives formal education."
2. Do you know anyone you think is a genius? What special qualities does he or she have?

Solve Some Puzzles

Try to answer these puzzles. Work with a partner.

1. Two U.S. coins equal thirty cents. One is not a quarter. What are the two coins?
2. A man walked into a pet shop and bought a parrot. The salesperson said the parrot would say everything it heard. However, the parrot never said a word. Why not?
3. Suppose you are driving from Philadelphia to Boston at a speed of 90 miles (145 kilometers) per hour. At the same time, your friend is driving from Boston to Philadelphia at a speed of 60 miles (97 kilometers) per hour. When the two cars meet, who is closer to Boston?
4. Two brothers were born on the same day, at the same time, in the same year, and at the same hospital. They have the same mother and father, but they are not twins. What are they?
5. A ship has a ladder on one side. There are 25 centimeters (10 inches) between each step. Ten steps of the ladder are underwater, and twenty steps are above water. If the water level goes down 75 centimeters (30 inches), how many steps will be outside the water?

How Good Is Your Memory?

Before You Read

A Discuss these questions with a partner.

1. Do you think you have a good memory or a bad memory? Why?
2. Look at the chart below. Which things are easy for you to remember? Which are hard? Check the correct box.

	Easy	Hard		Easy	Hard
people's names			dance steps		
people's faces			driving directions		
phone numbers			computer passwords		
birthdays			words to songs		

B Study these words from the interview. Complete the chart. Write each word next to the correct definition.

affect   complex   repeat

senses   stores

1.	puts something away until it is needed
2.	to say or do something again
3.	to produce a change in something or someone
4.	difficult to understand
5.	natural abilities such as seeing and hearing

✓ **Reading with a Purpose**

C You are going to read about memory. What are three things you hope to learn from the interview?

1. _____

2. _____

3. _____

How Good Is Your Memory?

1 **Interviewer:** What is memory?
Diane Englund: Memory is the ability to remember information and experiences. Memory is a **complex** topic. Scientists do not fully understand how memory works, but it is an important part of learning, thinking, and living. Your memory is like a system that organizes and **stores** everything you learn. Your **senses**—vision, hearing, touch, taste, and smell—help you receive and record the information. There are two kinds of memory: short-term and long-term.

2 **I:** What is the difference between short-term memory and long-term memory?
DE: Short-term memories are temporary. They are kept in your brain for only a few minutes. For example, a telephone number that you remember long enough to use is a short-term memory. You usually forget the number after you use it. Most people can only remember about seven items in order. That's why telephone numbers usually have seven numbers.

3 **I:** What about long-term memories?
DE: Long-term memories are stored in the brain for a long time. They are stronger than short-term memories. Long-term memories can last days, months, years, or even your whole life. For instance, the memory of how to ride a bike is a long-term memory. Memories of what you had for dinner last night, your first birthday

party, or your favorite song are also examples of long-term memories.

4 **I:** What things can affect memory?
DE: Several things can affect your memory. For example, when you are sick, very tired, or worried about something, it can be difficult to remember things. Age also affects your ability to remember. Younger people usually have better memories than older people.

5 **I:** Why do we forget things?
DE: No one has a perfect memory. Everyone forgets things. In fact, forgetting is a natural and necessary process. It is the way your brain makes room for more memories. Take reading, or listening to a lecture, for example. After one day, you will forget 46 percent of what you read or heard. After

Diane Englund is a teacher and therapist. She is interested in memory.

two weeks, you will forget 79 percent; after four weeks, you will forget 81 percent. How does this affect your study habits? Here's some advice: Review readings and lecture notes as soon as possible. Then review the information again.

6 **I:** How can you improve your memory?
DE: There are many books, videos, websites, and even classes about how to improve your memory. Each one suggests different ways to improve your memory. Some people even think certain foods or pills can strengthen your memory. I don't agree with that, but I do think it is possible to improve your memory. I believe that the more you practice a skill or review and **repeat** information, the better you remember it. ■

After You Read

Comprehension Check

A Read these statements. If a statement is true, write *T* on the line. If it is false, write *F*.

_____ 1. Your age and health can affect your ability to remember things accurately.

_____ 2. The two basic kinds of memory are short-term memory and long-term memory.

_____ 3. Short-term memories last a few days.

_____ 4. A memory of your first birthday party is an example of a long-term memory.

_____ 5. Practice and repetition can improve memory.

_____ 6. Taking pills will always improve your memory.

SKILL FOR SUCCESS ✓

Identifying Examples
Authors often use **examples** to explain or support their ideas.
The expressions *such as*, *for instance*, *for example*, and *like* introduce examples.

*Long-term memories can last for days, months, years, or even your whole life. **For instance,** the memory of how to ride a bike is a long-term memory.*

B Answer these questions. Write examples that Diane Englund used to explain her ideas.

1. What are some examples of your senses? _____

_____

2. What is an example of a short-term memory? _____

_____

3. What are some examples of long-term memories? _____

_____

4. What are some examples of things that affect your memory? _____

_____

Vocabulary Practice

A Complete each sentence with the correct word.

affect   complex   repeat
sense   stores

1. She wears glasses to improve her _____ of sight.

2. Most people agree that you remember information better if you

   _____ it.

3. Your long-term memory _____ information.

4. The human brain is a _____ part of the body.

5. Some people say what you eat can _____ your memory.

B Circle the correct answer.

1. Which can <u>affect</u> your weight?
   a. the kind of food you eat
   b. the kind of books you read

2. If you <u>repeat</u> the words to a poem, you _____.
   a. write them
   b. say them again

3. Which can <u>store</u> information?
   a. a computer
   b. a bicycle

4. Which of your <u>senses</u> lets you receive visual information?
   a. taste
   b. sight

5. A <u>complex</u> problem is _____.
   a. easy to solve
   b. difficult to solve

Learning Homonyms

Homonyms are words that are spelled the same but have different meanings. Homonyms are often also different parts of speech. For example:

*Many **stores** sell books about memory.* (In this sentence, *stores* is used as a noun and means *places where things are sold*.)

*Your memory organizes and **stores** everything you learn.* (In this sentence, *stores* is used as a verb and means *saves until you need it*.)

C Read these sentences. Write the meaning and part of speech of each underlined word. Use a dictionary to help you.

1. No one has a <u>perfect</u> memory.

   Meaning: _____*without any mistakes or problems*_____

   Part of speech: _____*adjective*_____

2. Some people think certain foods or pills can <u>perfect</u> your memory.

   Meaning: _____

   Part of speech: _____

3. I <u>sense</u> that you are feeling anxious about something.

   Meaning: _____

   Part of speech: _____

4. My <u>sense</u> of smell is getting worse as I get older.

   Meaning: _____

   Part of speech: _____

5. I don't want to watch this show. It's a <u>repeat</u> from last season.

   Meaning: _____

   Part of speech: _____

6. The more you <u>repeat</u> something, the better you will remember it.

   Meaning: _____

   Part of speech: _____

The average adult male brain weighs 3 pounds, 2.2 ounces (1.42 kilograms). The average female brain weighs 2 pounds, 6 ounces (1.08 kilograms). There is no connection between brain weight and intelligence.

Discuss these questions as a class.

1. Most people think it is wonderful to have a good memory, but there may be some things you wish you could forget. Do you have some memories you wish you could forget?
2. Is your memory as good as it was when you were younger?
3. Do you have any tricks you use to remember things? Explain them.

Tie It All Together

Discussion

Discuss these questions in a small group.

1. Have you ever forgotten an important date, such as a birthday or an anniversary? Describe what happened.
2. Thomas Edison is famous for inventing the electric lightbulb. He believed "Genius is 1 percent inspiration and 99 percent perspiration." What do you think he meant? Do you agree or disagree with him? Why?

Just for Fun

Try this brainteaser on some friends. Have them follow these steps:

1. Choose a number from 2 to 9, but don't say it out loud.
2. Multiply that number by 9.
3. Add the two digits of your answer together.
4. Subtract 5 from the answer.
5. Choose the letter of the English alphabet that your answer corresponds to. For example, 1 is *A,* 2 is *B,* and so on.
6. Think of a country that starts with that letter.
7. Take the second letter of the name of that country, and think of the biggest animal that starts with that letter.
8. Think of the color of that animal.
9. Tell the animal, color, and country that you are thinking of.

How many people answered "a gray elephant" and "Denmark"? Can you figure out why many people end up with these answers?

Video Activity

Memory Pill

This video is about a new pill that may help older people with memory problems. Do many older people have memory problems? Do you think this pill will be popular?

A Study these words and phrases. Then watch the video.

could not put my finger on it	magic bullet
medication	on the market
to slip (Her memory is slipping.)	treat

B Read these statements and then watch the video again. If a statement is true, write *T* on the line. If it is false, write *F*.

_____ 1. Nancy Dow is in good physical condition.

_____ 2. She has a good memory.

_____ 3. She will have surgery to fix her brain.

_____ 4. Drug companies are spending a lot of money to create the best memory pill.

_____ 5. There is only one new pill to help improve memory.

C Discuss these questions with a partner or in a small group.

1. Do you know any older people with memory problems? How do they feel about it?
2. Do you know of any natural ways to help improve memory?

Reader's Journal Think about the topics and ideas that you have read about and discussed in this unit. Choose a topic and write about it for ten to twenty minutes. Pick a topic from the following list, or choose one of your own.

- how to improve your memory
- your definition of a genius
- the differences between right-brained and left-brained people

Vocabulary Self-Test

Complete each sentence with the correct word.

A memorize   revolutionized   sense
  shy   specializes   verbal

1. Claudia doesn't like to go to parties. I think she is very

   _____ .

2. Harvey is a doctor. He _____ in heart disease.

3. Juliette has very good _____ skills. Although she is only
   two years old, she already speaks in complete sentences.

4. Computers have _____ our lives in many ways.

5. Some people find it difficult to _____ speeches. They
   need to use their notes.

6. I have a very good _____ of smell.

B creative   curious   genius
  logical   repeats   store

1. Samuel is a _____ at doing crossword puzzles. He can
   complete them very quickly.

2. Children are often like cats. They are _____ , and
   sometimes it gets them into trouble.

3. Georgette _____ the same stories again and again.
   I wish she would tell some new ones.

4. In the summer, I _____ my winter clothes in a box.

5. Hao is a musician. He also likes to paint and write poetry. All his

   friends think he is a very _____ person.

6. Hani is left-brained. He is a mathematician, and his thinking is

   always very _____ .

C affects   complex   experiments
immigrated   suddenly   visual

1. Painting is one of the _____ arts.

2. Engineers know how to solve _____ mathematical problems.

3. The Antonellis _____ to the United States from Italy.

4. We do a lot of _____ in physics class.

5. The rain began so _____ that we didn't have time to get inside before we got wet.

6. The disease _____ his ability to breathe.

COMPANIES THAT CARE

For some companies, making money is not the only goal. Other goals include helping the environment and improving society. In this unit, you will read about three companies that have achieved important environmental and social goals.

Points to Ponder

Think about these questions and discuss them in a small group.

1. Do you think businesses should be involved in social or political issues? Why or why not?

2. How can businesses help or hurt the communities they operate in?

3. Do you know of any companies that help the environment? How do they help it?

The Body Shop: A Success Story

Before You Read

A Discuss these questions with a partner.

1. Do you know anyone who owns his or her own business? What kind of business is it?
2. What qualities are necessary for someone to have in order to be successful in business?

B Study these words from the article. Complete the chart. Write each word or phrase next to the correct definition.

ambitious   containers   disadvantaged

founder   manufactures   natural resources

1.	having problems, such as lack of money or education, that make it difficult to succeed
2.	things such as land, plants, and oil that exist in nature and can be used by people
3.	someone who starts a business, organization, school, etc.
4.	uses machines to make things in large numbers
5.	things you can fill, such as boxes and bottles
6.	having a strong desire to be successful

C Make some predictions about the article. Think about the title and the headings. Look at the pictures, and read the captions. Make a list of your predictions.

_____

_____

_____

The Body Shop: A Success Story

The Birth of the Body Shop

Anita Roddick, founder of The Body Shop, was one of the most successful businesswomen in the world.

....

1 Anita Roddick was the **founder** of The Body Shop, a company that sells products for skin and hair. Roddick was a teacher before she opened The Body Shop in 1976. She didn't know anything about beauty products, but she had good ideas. She was **ambitious,** and her business grew quickly. Soon, Roddick became an international success. Today, The Body Shop has 2,000 stores in 50 countries. Roddick believed that businesses should do good things. That's why she dedicated her business to social and environmental change. Unfortunately, Roddick died in 2007, but her business continues.

Getting Ideas for Products

2 The Body Shop **manufactures** and sells over 600 different products. All of the products are made from natural ingredients. Roddick got ideas for her products from all over the world. She learned how people from traditional cultures used plants to take care of their bodies. In Sri Lanka, for example, she learned that women use fresh pineapple to make their skin soft. So, she created a face cream with pineapple. In Polynesia, she learned about cocoa butter. It makes your skin and hair soft. Cocoa Butter Hand and Body Lotion is one of The Body Shop's best-selling products. The company combines traditional ideas and modern technology to develop its products.

Protecting the Planet

3 The Body Shop believes in protecting the earth. It teaches its customers about environmental issues. It also makes business

decisions that protect **natural resources** and reduce waste[1]. For instance, The Body Shop's products are sold in **containers** made of a special plastic that creates less waste. The Body Shop is also against animal testing. It never tests its products or ingredients on animals.

The Body Shop sells all-natural products all over the world.

....

Helping Communities

4   The Body Shop also believes in helping **disadvantaged** communities around the world. For example, The Body Shop has a trade agreement with the Kayapo Indians of Brazil. The Kayapo grow Brazil nuts in the Amazon rain forest. The Body Shop buys these nuts to use in several products, such as a cream called Nut Body Butter. The trade agreements help communities earn money to improve education, build homes, and modernize farming. The Body Shop has similar trade agreements with communities in India, Mexico, Nepal, Tanzania, and Zambia.

5   Although some of Roddick's ideas for her company were unusual, they have been very successful. The Body Shop sells over $680 million in products a year! ■

[1] **waste** – things that are left after something has been used, or things that you do not want

After You Read

Comprehension Check

A   Read these statements. If a statement is true, write *T* on the line. If it is false, write *F*.

_____ 1. Anita Roddick studied business in school.

_____ 2. The Body Shop is a very successful business.

_____ 3. Many of the ideas for The Body Shop's products come from traditional cultures.

_____ 4. The Body Shop has trade agreements with many communities.

_____ 5. The Body Shop respects the environment.

_____ 6. The Body Shop tests its products on animals.

_____ 7. The Body Shop tries to use natural resources made of plastic.

_____ 8. Cocoa butter makes your skin and hair soft.

✓ Scanning for Information

B Scan the article for the answer to each question. Look for key words, numbers, and names to help you find the information. Work as quickly as possible.

1. When did the first Body Shop open? _____

2. How many Body Shop stores are there today? _____

3. How many countries have Body Shop stores? _____

4. How many kinds of products does The Body Shop sell?

   _____

5. Where did Anita Roddick learn about cocoa butter?

   _____

6. Where do the Kayapo Indians live? _____

Vocabulary Practice

A Complete each sentence with the correct word or phrase.

ambitious	container	disadvantaged
founder	manufactures	natural resources

1. Please put this cheese in a _____ so it stays fresh.

2. The Body Shop helps people who live in _____ communities.

3. He opened his business in 1990. He is the _____.

4. We shouldn't waste our _____.

5. Successful businesspeople are usually hardworking and

   _____.

6. My father's company _____ parts for cars.

B Circle the correct answer.

1. Which would you keep in a plastic <u>container</u>?
   a. fruit
   b. trees

2. An <u>ambitious</u> person wants to be _____.
   a. funny
   b. successful

3. Which are <u>natural resources</u>?
   a. oil and water
   b. clothes and shoes

4. Which can be <u>manufactured</u>?
   a. cars
   b. oceans

5. The <u>founder</u> of a business _____.
   a. was hired to work there
   b. started the business

✓ **Learning Synonyms and Antonyms**

C Decide if the following pairs of words are synonyms or antonyms. If they are synonyms, circle *S.* If they are antonyms, circle *A.*

1. reduce	increase	S	A
2. sell	buy	S	A
3. company	business	S	A
4. encourage	discourage	S	A
5. traditional	modern	S	A
6. founder	creator	S	A

Talk It Over

Discuss these questions as a class.

1. How did Anita Roddick get ideas for The Body Shop's products? Do you think this is a good way or a bad way? Why?
2. Do you like to use all-natural products? Why or why not?
3. Do you think trade agreements like those The Body Shop has are a good way to help communities?

126 UNIT 6

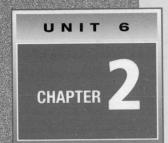

The Scoop on Ben & Jerry's

Before You Read

A Discuss these questions with a partner.

1. Do you like ice cream? Have you ever eaten Ben & Jerry's ice cream?
2. Have you ever made your own ice cream? What kinds have you made?
3. Have you heard of the Dave Matthews Band? Do you like their music?

B Study these words from the article. Complete the chart. Write each word next to the correct definition.

annually   charities   flavors

market   responsibility

1.	to encourage people to buy something
2.	once a year
3.	something that someone must do or take care of
4.	organizations that give money or help to people who need it
5.	the tastes of foods or drinks

✓ **Reading with a Purpose**

C You are going to read about Ben & Jerry's, a company that sells ice cream. What are three things you hope to learn from the article?

1. _____

2. _____

3. _____

THE SCOOP ON BEN & JERRY'S

Old Friends with a New Idea

1   Ben Cohen and Jerry Greenfield are the founders of a very successful ice-cream company. Ben and Jerry have been friends since 1963, when they were in junior high school. In 1977, they decided to start an ice-cream business together. They took a $5 course to learn how to make ice cream. Then they opened their first ice-cream shop in Burlington, Vermont, in 1978. They called it Ben & Jerry's Homemade Ice-Cream Shop.

A Great Ice-Cream Team

2   Ben and Jerry were a great team. They had creative ideas and worked well together. Jerry's job was to make the ice cream, and Ben's job was to sell and **market** it. They experimented to create unusual **flavors.** Ben and Jerry figured out the secret to making great ice cream. They started with fresh milk and cream and added natural flavorings and lots of big pieces of nuts, candy, fruit, and cookies. They used only the best ingredients to make their ice cream. The result was a fantastic product. Ben and Jerry had a plan to get people to try their product. They gave out free samples of ice cream everywhere they went. Their plan worked. The more ice cream they gave away, the more new customers they got. Ben and Jerry's ice cream was delicious. It became very popular, very fast. Today the company makes over 50 different kinds of ice cream and other products.

Unusual Goals

3   Ben and Jerry had business goals that were different from the goals of most other businesses. Most businesses have one main goal: to make a lot of money. Ben & Jerry's has three main goals. The first goal is to make great ice cream. The

Wavy Gravy is one of Ben & Jerry's most famous ice-cream flavors.

second is to make money. The third goal is to improve life locally, nationally, and internationally. Ben & Jerry's believes that business has a **responsibility** to the community and the environment. They give lots of ice cream to **charities,** homeless shelters[1], and community events. The company also gives $1.1 million dollars **annually** to support charities and issues such as world peace and protecting the environment.

Helping the Environment with Ice Cream and Music

4   One way Ben & Jerry's protects the environment is by trying to stop global warming[2]. They have joined with the Dave Matthews Band, a famous musical group, on a project called *Lick Global Warming*. The purpose of the project is to educate people about global warming and encourage them to take action against it. Ben & Jerry's created an ice-cream flavor called Dave Matthews Band's Magic Brownies. Part of the money they make from this flavor goes to stop global warming. *Lick Global Warming* is doing a great job. To learn more about it, visit the website **http://www. lickglobalwarming.org.**

---

[1] **homeless shelters** – places where people who don't have homes can live for a short time

[2] **global warming** – an increase in the earth's temperature caused by oil use and pollution

After You Read

A Check the topics discussed in the article.

❏ 1. how Ben and Jerry got people to try their product

❏ 2. the company's main goals

❏ 3. other companies that sell ice cream

❏ 4. examples of how the company is helping the environment

❏ 5. the company's history

❏ 6. the Dave Matthews Band's music

B Circle the correct answer.

1. Ben and Jerry became friends _____.
   a. when they were young students
   b. a few years ago
   c. when they started an ice-cream company

2. Ben & Jerry's ice cream _____ _____.
   a. took a long time to become popular
   b. became popular very quickly
   c. never became popular

3. Ben & Jerry's _____.
   a. has only one main goal
   b. has three main goals
   c. doesn't have any goals

4. *Lick Global Warming* is _____.
   a. the name of a song
   b. an ice-cream flavor
   c. a project to stop global warming

5. Ben and Jerry believe that all businesses _____.
   a. should care only about making money
   b. have a responsibility to the community and environment
   c. should give all their money to charities

F Y I

The average person in the United States eats about 32 quarts (34 liters) of ice cream per year.

Identifying Facts and Opinions
It is important to understand the difference between a **fact** and an **opinion**. A fact is something that you can show to be true. An opinion is someone's idea about something.

There are 30 students in our class. (fact)
The students are all very nice. (opinion)

C Decide if each statement is a fact or an opinion. Check the correct box.

	Fact	Opinion
1. Ben and Jerry opened their first ice-cream shop in 1978.	✓	
2. The result was a fantastic product.		✓
3. They experimented with new kinds of ice cream.	✓	
4. Ben & Jerry's gives $1.1 million a year to support the issues it believes in.	✓	
5. *Lick Global Warming* is doing a great job.		✓
6. Their ice cream was delicious.		✓
7. Today, the company makes over 50 different kinds of ice cream and other products.	✓	

Vocabulary Practice

A Complete each sentence with the correct word.

annually   charities   flavor
market   responsibility

1. My favorite _____ of Ben & Jerry's ice cream is Chocolate Fudge Brownie.

2. Ben had good ideas about how to _____ the ice cream.

3. The company gives lots of money to local _____.

4. Ben & Jerry's gives money _____ to support important issues. This year, it gave over $1 million.

5. We have a _____ to help the environment.

B Ask and answer these questions with a partner.

1. What is your favorite flavor of ice cream?
2. Do you give any money to charities? Which one or ones?
3. What is something you do annually?
4. What things do you feel a responsibility to do?
5. Was Ben and Jerry's idea to market their ice cream a good one? Why or why not?

✓ **Learning Homonyms**

C Read these sentences. Is the underlined word a noun or a verb? Check the correct box.

	Noun	Verb
1. Jerry's job was to make the ice cream, and Ben's job was to sell and market it.		✓
2. I buy vegetables at an outdoor market.	✓	
3. The old fruit had a bad taste.	✓	
4. Do you want to taste some of this ice cream?		✓
5. They only use the best ingredients to make their ice cream.		✓
6. What is the use of this tool?	✓	
7. They experiment with new flavors.		✓
8. The experiment turned out well.	✓	
9. I tried a delicious sample of ice cream at the store.	✓	
10. Do you want to sample this ice cream?		✓
11. Ben and Jerry had a plan to get people to try their product.	✓	
12. I plan to start school in the fall.		✓

Talk It Over

Discuss these questions as a class.

1. When Ben and Jerry first started their business they said, "If it's not fun, why do it?" Is this is a good or bad way to do business? Explain your answer.

2. Do you think companies have a responsibility to help save the environment? Why or why not?

Use Your Imagination

Work in a small group. Think of an idea for a new business. Answer these questions.

1. What is the name of the business? _____

2. What does the business sell or do? _____

_____

3. What are the goals? _____

_____

A New Use for Old Bottles

Before You Read

The sweater shown in this photo is made out of old soda bottles.

A Discuss these questions with a partner.

1. Sometimes the things people throw away can be made into new things and used again. Can you think of any examples of things that have been made from trash?
2. What do you do with your old clothes?
3. Look at the sweater in the photo. The sweater is made from trash! It was made from old plastic soda bottles. Would you buy a sweater made from old bottles?

B Study these words from the article. Complete the chart. Write each word or phrase next to the correct definition.

cloth   comfortable   give away

reuses   throw out

1.	to get rid of something because you do not want or need it anymore
2.	uses again
3.	a material used to make clothes, such as cotton or wool
4.	feeling good to wear (clothes) or sit in (furniture)
5.	to give something to someone without asking for payment

✓ **Thinking about What You Know**

C You are going to read an article about another company that cares about the environment. Check the statements you think are true about this topic.

❏ 1. Some businesses try to help the environment.

❏ 2. Plastic soda bottles are bad for the environment.

❏ 3. It is possible to make clothes out of plastic bottles.

❏ 4. Outdoor clothing is not comfortable.

❏ 5. People should give away their old clothes.

❏ 6. Most old soda bottles are reused.

✓ **Skimming for the Main Idea**

D Skim the article one time. Then choose the statement you think describes the main idea.

1. Lots of people buy too many clothes that they don't need.
2. Patagonia sells high-quality, comfortable clothes all over the world.
3. Patagonia helps the environment by making clothes out of old soda bottles.

A New Use for Old Bottles

1   Patagonia is a company that manufactures and sells outdoor clothes. The clothes are high in quality and **comfortable** to wear. They are also friendly to the environment. Yvon Chouinard is the founder of Patagonia. One of his goals was to make the best-quality product with the least amount of harm to the environment.

Reusing the Bottles

2   Do you drink soda from bottles? What do you do with the bottle after you finish your soda? If you are like many people, you **throw out** the bottle. That's bad for the environment. Every year, over 40 billion plastic bottles are produced in the United States alone. About 27 billion of them end up in the trash. That's *really* bad for the environment.

3   Patagonia is doing something creative to help solve the problem. It **reuses** the bottles that people throw out. It uses the old soda bottles to make new clothes. The idea to do this started in 1993 when Patagonia invented a new kind of **cloth** called Synchilla. The new cloth is woven from recycled[1] plastic soda bottles.

4   Synchilla is soft, yet strong. Patagonia uses Synchilla in over thirty-one products to make sweaters, pants, jackets, socks, baby clothes, hats, and much more. By using Synchilla, Patagonia has saved about 86 million soda bottles from the trash. That's good for the environment.

5   Patagonia uses twenty-five 2-liter bottles to make each Synchilla sweater. This means that for each Synchilla sweater Patagonia makes, twenty-five fewer soda bottles go into the trash. In addition, it takes less energy and fewer natural resources to make Synchilla cloth than it does to make other kinds of cloth.

You Can Help, Too

6   Patagonia hopes that its customers will do their part in helping the environment, too. Patagonia encourages people to recycle clothes they don't need. The company wants people to **give away** old clothes, not throw them out. There are many people around the world who need them. Clothes should be recycled and reused

---

[1] **recycled** – made into something new and used again

After You Read

Comprehension Check

A Read these statements. If a statement is true, write *T* on the line. If it is false, write *F*.

_____ 1. Synchilla is made from recycled plastic soda bottles.

_____ 2. Patagonia makes formal clothing.

_____ 3. Synchilla is only used to make sweaters.

_____ 4. It takes more energy to make Synchilla than it does to make other kinds of cloth.

_____ 5. Patagonia makes soda bottles.

_____ 6. Patagonia helps the environment.

✓ **Scanning for Information**

B Scan the article for the answer to each question. Look for key words, numbers, and names to help you find the information. Work as quickly as possible.

1. When did Patagonia first make Synchilla? _____

2. How many 2-liter bottles does it take to make one Synchilla sweater? _____

3. How many plastic bottles are produced each year in the United States? _____

4. How many of these bottles end up in the trash? _____

5. How many products is Synchilla used in? _____

6. How many soda bottles has Patagonia saved from the trash? _____

Vocabulary Practice

A Complete each sentence with the correct word or phrase.

cloth   comfortable   give away
reuses   throw out

1. This _____ is made out of cotton.

2. Patagonia _____ old soda bottles. It makes clothes out of them.

3. It's time to _____ this cheese. It smells bad.

4. I love to wear this sweater. It so soft and _____.

5. You should _____ your old books. Someone else will want to read them.

B Circle the correct answer.

1. Which would you <u>throw out</u>?

   a. old meat

   b. new shoes

2. Which is more <u>comfortable</u> to wear?

   a. a pair of jeans that are too small

   b. an old, soft pair of jeans

3. Which is used to make <u>cloth</u> for shirts?

   a. cotton

   b. books

4. Which should you <u>give away</u>?

   a. an old coat that doesn't fit you anymore

   b. a new coat that you just bought

5. If you <u>reuse</u> something, you _____.

   a. have never used it before

   b. have used it in the past

SKILL
FOR ✓
SUCCESS

Understanding Word Parts: The Prefix *re-*
The prefix *re-* is common in English. *Re-* is usually added to a verb to mean *to do again.* For example, the word *reuse* from the article means *use again.*

C Add the prefix *re-* to each word. Then write a sentence using the new word. Use your dictionary to help you.

1. ___*re*___arrange   *I will rearrange my bedroom furniture.*

2. _____read   _____

3. _____ marry _____

4. _____ decorate _____

5. _____ order _____

Pick a Business Card

Use the information on the business cards to answer the questions about each situation.

Computer Doctor

Taking care of all your computer needs

Justin Northrup
phone/fax: 617-555-1678
www.NorthrupCompDoc.com

Apple Tree Publishing Company

Eun Han, Editor, Poetry

36 Monroe Place
New York, NY 10012

Phone/fax:
212-555-1000,
Extension 2311

Dave Yoo

Private Tutoring in Math and Science

25 Windy Way
Gainesville, Florida 32611
Cell phone: 352-555-8369

ESL INK CANADA

Sara Ridley, Director

www.eslink.edu

Learn English with us!

301 North Street
Toronto, Ontario
M4B 1B3

Phone/fax:
416-555-1000,
Extension 2311

Campus Apartments

Fran Davis

209 Stetson Avenue
Portland, Oregon 97233

Cell: 503-555-9151

Shortman Publishing Group

Hasan Kara, Sales Representative
Textbook Order Department

Istanbul, Turkey
+90 213 555 4716

www.shortmanpubgroup.com

FOREIGN LANGUAGE INSTITUTE

Lina Morales

SPANISH TEACHER

141 Industry Avenue
San Antonio, Texas 78203
Lmorales@FLIhome.edu

210-555-5891

---

1. You are the director of an English language program in Istanbul. You want to order textbooks for your students. What number should you call? _____

2. Your son was sick and missed a week of school. Now he is having trouble in math class. Who can help him? _____

3. You just got a new job, and you will have to travel frequently to Mexico. You want to learn some Spanish before you go. What address should you e-mail? _____

4. You just moved to Canada and need to take an ESL class to practice speaking, reading, and writing in English. What website should you visit? _____

5. Your computer stopped working last night while you were writing a term paper. You need to get it fixed right away. What number should you call? _____

6. You recently moved to Oregon to start college, and you need to rent an apartment. You want someone to show you some apartments that are available. Who should you call? _____

Use the Internet

Look up some facts about Patagonia on its website, www.patagonia.com. Make a list of five new things you learn about the company. Share your list with a partner.

1. _____

2. _____

3. _____

4. _____

5. _____

Tie It All Together

Discussion   Discuss these questions in a small group.

1. Anita Roddick has said, "A company that makes a profit from society has a responsibility to return something to that society." Do you agree or disagree? Why?
2. Have you ever had an idea that you thought would make a good business? Explain the idea.

Just for Fun   The word *responsibility* has fourteen letters. Use these letters to make as many other words as you can. You may not use the same letter twice unless it appears twice in the word *responsibility*. Do not use names or foreign words.

_____*tie*_____   _____   _____

_____   _____   _____

_____   _____   _____

_____   _____   _____

_____   _____   _____

_____   _____   _____

_____   _____   _____

_____   _____   _____

abc NEWS

Video Activity   **Giving Back Big**

This video is about what Bill Gates and other professionals in Seattle, Washington, are doing with their money. What do you know about Bill Gates?

A   Study these words and phrases. Then watch the video.

fortunes   high-tech revolution   next generation

philanthropist   retire   share their wealth

specific causes

B Read these questions and then watch the video again. Write an answer to each question.

1. What is the Bill and Melinda Gates Foundation? _____

    _____

2. Who are the high-tech philanthropists and how are they unique? ____

    _____

3. What is Trish Millines doing with her money? _____

    _____

4. What is Paul Brainerd doing with his money? _____

    _____

C Discuss these questions with a partner or in a small group.

1. List some charities or causes that you know of. Which are the most important to you?
2. Do you think all wealthy people should give some of their money to a charity or cause?

Reader's Journal   Think about the topics and ideas you have read about and discussed in this unit. Choose a topic and write about it for ten to twenty minutes. Pick a topic from the following list, or choose one of your own.

- an unusual business idea that you know about
- socially conscious businesses in your country
- the qualities of a successful businessperson

Circle the correct answer.

1. Which of these is a <u>container</u>?
   a. a box
   b. an apple
   c. a chair

2. If you do something <u>annually</u>, how often do you do it?
   a. once a week
   b. once a day
   c. once a year

3. Which of these is a type of <u>cloth</u>?
   a. cotton
   b. candy
   c. flowers

4. A <u>flavor</u> is something you _____.
   a. taste
   b. smell
   c. see

5. The purpose of a <u>charity</u> is to _____ to help people.
   a. take money
   b. give money
   c. make money

6. Which of these can you <u>reuse</u>?
   a. clothes
   b. gas
   c. milk

7. If you want to <u>market</u> something, you want to _____.
   a. buy it
   b. look at it
   c. sell it

8. If you are <u>ambitious</u>, you _____.
   a. have to succeed
   b. want to succeed
   c. don't want to succeed

9. If a community is <u>disadvantaged</u>, it _____.
   a. has no problems
   b. has fewer problems than usual
   c. has more problems than usual

10. If your shoes are <u>comfortable</u>, they are _____.
    a. too big
    b. too small
    c. just right

11. When you <u>manufacture</u> something, you _____.
    a. make it in large numbers
    b. make it in small numbers
    c. make it by hand

12. Which of these is not a <u>natural resource</u>?
    a. books
    b. oil
    c. trees

13. If you <u>give away</u> your pencil, you _____.
    a. let someone have it
    b. let someone buy it
    c. let someone borrow it

14. If you feel a <u>responsibility</u>, you feel _____.

    a. a cloth

    b. a duty to do something

    c. a flavor

15. If you are the <u>founder</u> of a company, you _____.

    a. work for the company

    b. buy from the company

    c. started the company

16. Which of these should you **NOT** <u>throw out</u>?

    a. money

    b. trash

    c. old food

FOOD FOR THOUGHT

English speakers use the expression *food for thought* to describe something that is worth thinking about. We hope the chapters in this unit will give you food for thought.

Points to Ponder

Think about these questions and discuss them in a small group.

1. What is your favorite meal: breakfast, lunch, or dinner?

2. Do you like to try food from different countries? Why or why not?

3. What is your favorite food?

Space Muffin Wins Contest

Before You Read

A Discuss these questions with a partner.

1. Do you like to cook? Do you ever create your own dishes?
2. What kind of food do you think is eaten on flights into space?

B Study these words from the article. Complete the chart. Write each word or phrase next to the correct definition.

astronauts   judge   nutritious
out of this world   prepare   snack

1.	very good
2.	people who travel and work in space
3.	a small amount of food that you eat between meals
4.	to decide who will be the winner of a contest
5.	healthful
6.	to make or get something ready to be used

✓ **Predicting**

C Make some predictions about the article. Think about the title and the headings. Look at the picture, and read the caption. Make a list of your predictions.

_____

_____

_____

Space Muffin Wins Contest

A New Muffin for Hungry Astronauts

1   A group of students at Oklahoma State University created a new muffin for hungry **astronauts** to eat in space. Their new muffin is **out of this world**! The students named the muffin *Nutraffin* because it combines the words *nutritious* and *muffin*. The bite-size muffin was entered in the 2005 NASA Space-Travel Food Contest. It won first prize!

2   The students' healthy muffin is made of carrots, soymilk, peanuts, and wheat flour. It is high in protein and vitamins, and it's low in salt. The muffin has a lot of calories, to give astronauts an energy boost. It will be a great **snack** for space flights. Cheryll Reitmeier is coordinator of the contest. She said, "Nutraffin is an interesting product and has a great potential for future space flight."

About the Contest

3   The nationwide space-food contest was started in 2001. It takes place every year at the NASA Food Technology Space Center at Iowa State University. The purpose of the contest is for students to learn about food that can be used for long-term space travel. Here are some of the rules of the contest. The food must be nutritious, easy to **prepare**, and safe to eat. It must be made from plants that astronauts can grow on the spacecraft. And, of course, the food should taste good. Food scientists from NASA **judge** the contest and choose the winner.

Nutraffins are mini-size snacks for space travel.

....

4   The winner last year was a product called Veg@eez. It is a three-layer vegetable spread. In 2003, the contest winner was Pizza Poppers. Pizza Poppers are snack-size pizzas that come in three flavors.

Will the Nutraffin Take Off?

5   Some award-winning foods never make it into space. But the Oklahoma team hopes NASA will add Nutraffin to the list of foods that astronauts eat. The students will present Nutraffin to NASA food scientists this fall. ■

After You Read

Comprehension Check

Read these statements. If a statement is true, write *T* on the line. If it is false, write *F*.

_____ 1. Astronauts created Nutraffin.

_____ 2. Nutraffin is high in calories.

_____ 3. Nutraffin won the space-food competition.

_____ 4. The purpose of the space-food competition is to make money.

_____ 5. The food products must be easy to make.

_____ 6. Last year's contest winner was Pizza Poppers.

_____ 7. All winning foods make it into space.

Vocabulary Practice

A Complete each sentence with the correct word or phrase.

astronaut	judge	nutritious
out of this world	prepare	snack

1. Two teachers are going to _____ the essay contest and pick a winner.

2. Neil Armstrong is a famous _____. He was the first person to walk on the moon.

3. Students must _____ a food that can be eaten on a spacecraft.

4. Vegetables and fruits are _____ foods. They are very good for you.

5. This cake is _____! Please give me another piece.

6. We aren't going to eat until 9:00 tonight. Do you want a

   _____ before dinner?

B Circle the correct answer.

1. Which is a <u>snack</u>?

   a. a small muffin

   b. a big dinner

2. What do <u>astronauts</u> travel in?

   a. large boats

   b. spacecraft

3. If you think something you are eating is <u>out of this world</u>, you _____.

   a. don't really like it

   b. like it very much

4. Which would a person be asked to <u>judge</u>?

   a. an essay contest

   b. a telephone call

5. Which would you <u>prepare</u>?

   a. snow

   b. a meal

6. Which is <u>nutritious</u>?

   a. a piece of cake

   b. an apple

SKILL FOR SUCCESS

Learning Compound Words

A compound word is made of two or more words. For example, *spacecraft* and *bite-size* are compound words.

When a compound word is used as an adjective and comes before a noun, the word is often hyphenated.

   *The **bite-size** muffin was created for hungry astronauts.*

C Find these compound words in the article. Can you guess what they mean?

Paragraph 1: bite-size
Paragraph 2: soymilk
Paragraph 3: long-term, nationwide, spacecraft, space-food
Paragraph 4: three-layer, snack-size
Paragraph 5: award-winning

D Complete each sentence with the correct compound word.

award-winning   bite-size   long-term
nationwide   soymilk   spacecraft
three-layer

1. The baby is allergic to regular milk, so she drinks
   _____ .

2. The movie has won many prizes. The _____ movie is
   in theaters now.

3. She cut the chicken up into _____ pieces for
   her child.

4. The _____ has enough room for three astronauts.

5. I bought a _____ cake for her birthday party. One
   layer was chocolate, and the other two were lemon.

6. The telephone service has a _____ network. You can
   call anywhere in the country.

7. He has a good _____ memory.

Create a Menu

Astronauts eat three meals a day: breakfast, lunch, and dinner. Work in
a small group to make a sample menu for one day on a spacecraft.
Remember the foods must be nutritious, easy to prepare, safe to eat,
and tasty. Also, they should not be messy to eat.

Breakfast	Lunch	Dinner

Chocolate: A Taste of History

Before You Read

A Discuss these questions with a partner.

1. Do you like chocolate? How often do you eat it?
2. What foods and drinks are made with chocolate in your country?

B Study these words from the article. Complete the chart. Write each word next to the correct definition.

beverage   delicious   explorers
respect   spicy   treats

1.	things that you enjoy, especially to eat
2.	a good opinion of or admiration for someone
3.	a drink
4.	tasting very good
5.	having a strong, hot taste
6.	people who travel to unknown places to find out about them

✓ Thinking about What You Know

C You are going to read an article about chocolate. Check the statements you think are true about chocolate.

❑ 1. Chocolate is a new kind of food.

❑ 2. Chocolate was discovered about 500 years ago.

❑ 3. Chocolate is made from beans of a cocoa tree.

❑ 4. Chocolate is only popular in a few countries.

❑ 5. Chocolate was first used as a drink.

❑ 6. Today, chocolate comes in many forms.

Chocolate: A Taste of History

1 Chocolate is one of the world's favorite foods. But did you know that people have been eating chocolate for over a thousand years? The Museum of Natural History in New York City had an exhibit celebrating the history of chocolate. It was called *All about Chocolate*. Charles Spencer works at the museum. He said, "Chocolate is a gift from Latin America to the rest of the world."

A Long History

2 Visitors to the exhibit learned all about the history of chocolate. More than 1,500 years ago, the Mayan people of Central America discovered how to make chocolate. They made it from the beans of cocoa trees. They used the seeds to make a **spicy**, hot drink. The chocolate **beverage** was used in religious and royal ceremonies. When a king died, a cup of the chocolate drink was buried with him as a sign of **respect**.

3   Many years later, in the 1400s, the Aztecs ruled much of Mexico and Central America. They used cocoa beans as money. Why did they use cocoa beans? The beans were small and easy to carry around. Cocoa beans were also rare. This made them valuable. It cost 100 beans to purchase a slave. A turkey cost ninety cocoa beans, and a small rabbit cost thirty beans. Back then, money really did grow on trees!

4   Then, in the 1500s, Spanish **explorers** arrived in the New World. This was the first time that Europeans tasted chocolate. They mixed it with sugar and thought it tasted **delicious.** They liked chocolate so much that they brought it back to Europe with them.

Chocolate Today

5   Visitors to the exhibit also learned about chocolate today. Now cocoa beans are grown mostly in West Africa and South America. After the beans are dried, they are sent to chocolate makers in the United States and Europe. Some of the world's finest chocolate is made in Belgium, France, and Switzerland.

6   Today, chocolate is one of the most popular **treats** in the world. And now it comes in all shapes and sizes. People eat chocolate candy, chocolate cake, and chocolate cookies. They also drink cold chocolate milk, hot chocolate, and chocolate soda. You can get chocolate in boxes, bottles, or cones. Which country enjoys chocolate the most? Switzerland does. People there eat lots of chocolate. About 28 pounds (2.7 kilograms) of chocolate is eaten per person every year in Switzerland!

Good, and Good for You

7   Since most chocolate is made with unhealthful fat and lots of sugar, you have probably heard that it's bad for you. But here is some good news: Some chocolate may actually be good for you! Doctors think dark chocolate may have health benefits. A recent study showed that dark chocolate may be good for your heart. Isn't that sweet news?

After You Read

A Read these statements. If a statement is true, write _T_ on the line. If it is false, write _F_.

_____ 1. The Maya discovered chocolate.

_____ 2. Chocolate is made from the beans of cocoa trees.

_____ 3. The Maya used a chocolate drink in religious and royal ceremonies.

_____ 4. Cocoa beans were once used as money by Europeans.

_____ 5. Europeans first tasted chocolate thousands of years ago.

_____ 6. Today, some of the world's most popular chocolate is made in Mexico.

_____ 7. The Swiss eat a lot of chocolate.

_____ 8. Chocolate may help fight heart disease.

✓ **Recognizing Time Order**

B Number these events so they are in the correct time order.

_____ The Aztecs used cocoa beans as money.

_____ Today, cocoa beans are grown mostly in West Africa and South America.

_____ The Maya discovered chocolate.

_____ Spanish explorers arrived in the New World in the 1500s, and Europeans first tasted chocolate.

Vocabulary Practice

A Complete each sentence with the correct word.

beverage	delicious	explorer
respect	spicy	treat

1. Gabriel García Márquez was a very talented writer. I have great

_____ for his skill.

2. I can't eat _____ food. It gives me a stomachache.

3. Vasco da Gama was a Portuguese _____ who discovered a way to sail from Portugal to Asia.

4. It's so hot today. I'd love a cold _____ to drink.

5. This is the best meal I have ever eaten. It's _____.

6. I gave my son a piece of chocolate candy for a _____.

B Circle the correct answer.

1. Which food is <u>spicy</u>?
   a. a bowl of chili with hot peppers
   b. a piece of bread with butter

2. Which is a <u>beverage</u>?
   a. a chocolate cake
   b. a cup of coffee

3. Which is a <u>treat</u>?
   a. a piece of candy
   b. medicine for a cold

4. If something is <u>delicious</u>, you would probably _____.
   a. want to eat it
   b. want to read about it

5. If you <u>respect</u> someone, you _____.
   a. don't like him or her
   b. have a good opinion of him or her

6. An <u>explorer</u> likes to _____.
   a. stay at home
   b. travel to new places

SKILL FOR SUCCESS ✓

Understanding Word Parts: The Suffixes -*er* and -*or*

Two common **suffixes** are -*er* and -*or*. They mean *someone who does something*.

explore → explorer (someone who explores)

direct → director (someone who directs)

The average person in the United States eats about 12 pounds (5.5 kilograms) of chocolate each year.

C Complete each sentence with a word that ends in the suffix -*er* or -*or*. Use your dictionary to help you.

1. Someone who acts in movies is an _____.

2. Someone who illustrates books is an _____.

3. Someone who manages a business is a _____.

4. Someone who dances is a _____.

5. Someone who takes photographs is a _____.

6. Someone who visits your home is a _____.

Talk It Over

Discuss these questions as a class.

1. What is your favorite way to eat or drink chocolate?
2. The Maya and Aztecs used chocolate for money. Do you know what the people in your country used for money many years ago?

Take a Survey

Ask five people to tell you their favorite and least favorite flavors of ice cream. Record their answers in the chart. Share your survey results with your classmates. What was the most popular flavor? The least popular?

Name	Favorite Flavor	Least Favorite Flavor

Do TV Commercials Affect Eating Habits?

Before You Read

A Discuss these questions with a partner.

1. Do you like watching the commercials on TV? Do you think they give helpful information? Are they interesting?
2. Do you have a favorite TV commercial? What is it?
3. Have you ever bought any products because you saw them marketed on TV?

B Study these words from the article. Complete the chart. Write each word next to the correct definition.

advertise   fast food   kids

overweight   underweight

1.	children
2.	weighing too little
3.	to give information about a product so people will buy it
4.	food that is made and served quickly
5.	weighing too much

✓ **Skimming for the Main Idea**

C Skim the article one time. Then choose the statement you think describes the main idea.

1. Children like to eat while they watch TV.
2. Television commercials affect the eating habits of children.
3. Overweight children watch too much TV.

DO TV COMMERCIALS AFFECT EATING HABITS?

1 Do television commercials influence the eating habits of children? A new study by the Kaiser Family Foundation says yes. According to the study, food commercials influence what **kids** want to eat and often encourage them to eat unhealthy foods. These poor food choices can lead to weight gain, a growing problem for children across the United States.

2 A typical American child sees about 40,000 commercials a year. That's almost 110 a day. These commercials usually **advertise** soda, cereal, candy, and **fast food**. They often influence children to eat more of these unhealthy foods.

TV commercials often influence kids to eat unhealthy foods.

3 To get children's attention, commercials sometimes use popular movie or cartoon characters that children love. These commercials confuse kids about the health benefits of certain foods. As a result, children may think the foods they are eating are healthy.

4 Many children in the United States are **overweight**. The percentage of young people ages 6 to 11 who are overweight has more than doubled since 1980. Today, 30 percent of people in this age group are overweight. Doctors are worried about these numbers because being overweight can lead to other health problems, such as heart disease and diabetes. Can TV commercials affect weight gain? "While the media are only one of many factors that appear to be affecting childhood obesity[1], it's an important piece of the puzzle," said Vicky Rideout, vice president and director of the Kaiser Family Foundation.

5 Although overweight kids have gotten a lot of media attention, many kids maintain a healthy weight, and some suffer from another problem: being **underweight**. What should kids do to maintain a healthy weight and lifestyle? Experts suggest children talk with their parents and doctors to make sure that they are eating a healthy, balanced diet and getting enough exercise.

[1] **obesity** – the condition of being very overweight

After You Read

A Circle the correct answer.

1. A new study by the Kaiser Family Foundation says _____.
   a. children should talk to their parents about eating healthy foods
   b. television commercials influence the eating habits of children

2. Some commercials use _____ to get children's attention.
   a. experts on nutrition
   b. popular cartoon characters

3. According to Vicky Rideout, commercials are _____.
   a. the only thing that affects children's eating habits
   b. one of many things that affect childhood obesity

4. TV commercials can confuse children about _____.
   a. the health benefits of certain foods
   b. the problems of being underweight

5. Being overweight can lead to _____.
   a. more TV commercials
   b. other health problems

6. The author of the reading thinks that soda and candy are
   _____.
   a. good for you
   b. unhealthy

Making Inferences

An **inference** is a guess or conclusion based on information you hear or read and information you already know. Learning to make inferences will make you a better reader.

B Check the statements that are inferences you can make based on the information in the article.

❑ 1. Eating too much fast food is not good for children.

❑ 2. Most TV commercials are for children.

❑ 3. All actors eat unhealthy food.

❑ 4. Children are influenced by movie stars and cartoon characters they love.

❑ 5. Obesity among children is increasing.

❑ 6. Heart disease and diabetes are the only health problems being overweight can cause.

❑ 7. Parents and doctors can help kids make healthy choices.

✓ **Scanning for Information**

C Scan the article for the answer to each question. Look for key words, numbers, and names to help you find the information. Work as quickly as possible.

1. How many commercials does the typical American child see per year? _____

2. How much has the percentage of overweight children between the ages of 6 and 11 increased since 1980? _____

3. What percent of children are overweight? _____

4. Who is the vice president and director of the Kaiser Family Foundation? _____

A Complete each sentence with the correct word or phrase.

advertise   fast food   kids
overweight   underweight

1. I am very busy, but I try not to eat too much _____.

2. Children who are _____ need to lose weight.

3. _____ people need to gain weight.

4. Mrs. Lee only lets her _____ watch an hour of TV a day.

5. Companies like to _____ their products on TV.

B Cross out the word in each group that does not belong.

1. advertise   market   return
2. thin   underweight   fat
3. overweight   heavy   skinny
4. adults   kids   children

SKILL FOR SUCCESS ✓

Learning Compound Words with *Over* and *Under*
The words *over* and *under* are often combined with other words to form compound words.

When *over* is used to make a compound word, it often means *too much*. For example, *overcharge* means *charge too much money*.

When *under* is used to make a compound word, it often means *too little*. For example, *undercharge* means *charge too little money*.

C Use *over* or *under* to complete each sentence.

1. I left this fish in the oven too long. I _____ cooked it.

2. He didn't pay me enough for my work. He _____ paid me.

3. The baby shouldn't be wearing such a heavy sweater on a warm day.
   She is _____ dressed.

4. Look at the bill. I was charged too much for this meal. I was
   _____ charged.

5. The children don't get enough to eat. They are getting sick because
   they are _____ fed.

Read the advertisements. Then answer the questions that follow.

LINCOLN STREET DELI

STARTED IN 1900 AND STILL POPULAR

Family owned

the best food at the best prices

OPEN 24 HOURS

52 Chestnut Street
949-555-6761

ROOM 222

Fast, delicious food
served with a smile

CONVENIENT DOWNTOWN LOCATION

Open 7 A.M.-10 P.M.

949-555-2222   222 Center Street

The Blue Lobster

Let us serve you our fine, fresh
seafood as you enjoy our
beautiful ocean scenery.

*Open daily
for lunch and dinner.*

**Live music Sunday and
Monday nights 6-10 P.M.**

Reservations accepted for groups of 6 or more.

123 Atlantic Avenue   949-555-BLUE

TREATS

We use only the best ingredients
to make our rich, creamy,
and delicious desserts.

If you like sweets, you'll love TREATS!

Eat here or take out.
Open daily 5-10 P.M. Bakery open 12-5 P.M.

369 Packard Street   949-555-6304

Maria's Cafe

Enjoy our flavorful cooking as you relax.

Outdoor seating available in good weather

Monday-Saturday 11:30 A.M. to 11 P.M.
Sunday 10 A.M. to 10 P.M.

7575 8th Street   949-555-5346

1. Martina works downtown. She didn't have time for lunch today, and she is hungry. She wants to get something quick and easy before she goes home. Where should she go?

   _____

2. Brigitte and Carolina have been studying hard for a big test. Now they want something sweet to eat. Where should they go?

   _____

3. Sen had to stay up late to write a term paper. It's now 2:00 in the morning, and he is really hungry. Where can he get something to eat?

   _____

4. Kiko and her daughter have been shopping. It's such a beautiful day that they want to eat lunch at an outdoor café. Where can they go?

   _____

5. Mark wants to take Cyndi to a nice restaurant to celebrate her birthday. She loves seafood. Which restaurant should they go to?

   _____

Create a Commercial

Work in a small group to create a TV commercial about a food product. Think of a food you want to advertise. Write the commercial and give each person in your group a part in it. Present your commercial to the class.

Discussion

Discuss these questions in a small group.

1. What are some of the ways that food is important in our lives (other than to keep us alive)?
2. What can you learn about a culture by studying its food and eating habits?
3. What do you think the author George Bernard Shaw meant when he said, "There is no love sincerer than the love of food"?
4. "Food is our common ground, a universal experience." Discuss this quote with your classmates. How is this statement true or untrue for your class?

Just for Fun

Below is a list of questions. Each one refers to something we eat. Write the correct answers on the lines. The last letter of each answer will always be the first letter of the next answer. Work in a small group.

Examples:

a. What is made from the beans of cocoa trees?

  c h o c o l a t e

b. What can you scramble, boil, or fry for breakfast?

  e g g s

c. What do you eat between meals?

  s n a c k s

1. What do we make when we mix lettuce, tomatoes, cucumbers, carrots, and other vegetables together?

  __ __ __ __ __ __

2. What is the name for something sweet we eat after a meal?

  __ __ __ __ __ __ __

3. What is the name for an Asian sauce often served on meat?

  __ __ __ __ __ __ __ __

4. What is a frozen dessert that comes in many flavors?

  __ __ __ __ __ __ __ __

5. What do vegetarians not eat?

  __ __ __ __

6. What hot beverage do British and Asian people drink a lot of?

   __ __ __

7. What is a thick-skinned, green-colored fruit that is especially popular in Mexico?

   __ __ __ __ __ __ __

8. What fruit is often made into a breakfast drink?

   __ __ __ __ __ __

9. What do we make omelets out of?

   __ __ __ __

10. What is a popular pasta often served with tomato sauce?

   __ __ __ __ __ __ __ __ __

Video Activity

Sugar and Kids

This video explains how sugar affects children. What do you think you will learn?

A Study these words and phrases. Then watch the video.

act up	calm down	go crazy
go nuts	hyper	myth
off the wall	studies (noun)	sugar high/crash mode

B Read these statements and then watch the video again. Choose the statement that describes the main idea.

1. Children and teenagers love sugar and how they feel when they eat it.
2. Sugar is bad for children's health.
3. Research says that sugar does not make kids hyper.

C Discuss these questions with a partner or in a small group.

1. Do you eat a lot of sugar? What kinds of sweet food do you like?
2. How does sugar affect you?
3. Are there any foods that make you feel very tired? Hyper? Calm? Strong? Which foods are they?

Reader's Journal Think about the topics and ideas you have read about and discussed in this unit. Choose a topic and write about it for ten to twenty minutes. Pick a topic from the following list, or choose one of your own.

- the best or worst meal you have ever eaten
- why you like or don't like to try food from different countries
- ways to have a healthy diet

Vocabulary Self-Test

Read and answer each question. Check *Yes* or *No.* Then discuss your responses as a class.

1. If something is <u>out of this world</u>, is it bad?
   ❏ yes　　　　　❏ no

2. If you do not like <u>spicy</u> food, would you like salsa?
   ❏ yes　　　　　❏ no

3. If you think something is <u>delicious</u>, do you like it?
   ❏ yes　　　　　❏ no

4. If you <u>prepare</u> dinner, do you go to a restaurant?
   ❏ yes　　　　　❏ no

5. If you <u>respect</u> someone, do you have a bad opinion of him or her?
   ❏ yes　　　　　❏ no

6. If you are trying to sell a product, should you <u>advertise</u> it?
   ❏ yes　　　　　❏ no

7. If you were thirsty, would you like a <u>beverage</u>?
   ❏ yes　　　　　❏ no

8. If you go to a place to find out about it, are you an <u>explorer</u>?
   ❏ yes　　　　　❏ no

9. Do you think doctors would encourage eating <u>nutritious</u> food?
   ❏ yes　　　　　❏ no

10. Should <u>overweight</u> people eat a lot of candy?
    ❏ yes　　　　　❏ no

11. Does <u>fast food</u> take a long time to make?
    ❏ yes　　　　　❏ no

12. Do you weigh too much if you are <u>underweight</u>?
    ❏ yes　　　　　❏ no

13. Do <u>astronauts</u> study the ocean?

☐ yes ☐ no

14. Is a large dinner a <u>snack</u>?

☐ yes ☐ no

15. When someone <u>judges</u> something, does he give his opinion?

☐ yes ☐ no

16. Is homework an example of a <u>treat</u>?

☐ yes ☐ no

17. Are <u>kids</u> younger than adults?

☐ yes ☐ no

HOW'S THE WEATHER?

Climate and weather affect many areas of our lives. The types of houses we build, the kinds of clothes we wear, the way we spend our free time, the kinds of food we eat, and even the development of countries are all influenced by climate.

Stephen O. Muskie/www.cuttakes.com

Points to Ponder

Answer these questions. Then discuss your answers in a small group.

1. What is your favorite season? Why?

2. Does the weather affect your mood? How?

3. What kinds of weather can you name? Make a list.

Are You SAD?

Before You Read

A Think about how you feel when the seasons change. Complete the chart. Check *Yes* or *No*. Then compare answers with a partner.

When the seasons change . . .	Yes	No
do you have less energy than usual?		
do you feel less creative?		
do you feel sad or depressed?		
do you need more sleep than usual?		
do your eating habits change?		
are you less productive?		

B Study these words from the article. Complete the chart. Write each word next to the correct definition.

artificial   concentrate   depressed   mild   stress

1.	not natural; made by people
2.	very sad
3.	the feeling of being worried because of difficulties in your life
4.	to think very carefully about something you are doing
5.	not too strong or serious

✓ **Skimming for the Main Idea**

C Skim the article one time. Then choose the statement you think describes the main idea.

1. People with SAD can't concentrate well.
2. Many people suffer from SAD when the seasons change.
3. People who have SAD should stay in air-conditioned places.

Are You SAD?

1 The weather affects everyone, but some people react to changes in the weather more than others. For several years, doctors have been studying people who become **depressed** when the seasons change. These people suffer from Seasonal Affective Disorder, or SAD. Some people have a **mild** form of SAD, which does not affect their lives very much. But, other people have a more serious form. When the seasons change, they become very depressed.

Who Suffers from SAD?

2 Millions of people have SAD. It affects more women than men, usually adults between the ages of 20 and 40. However, SAD can affect children, too. People who live in cold climates are more likely to have SAD than people who live in warm climates.

Why Do People Get SAD?

3 Scientists are trying to understand the causes of SAD. They think the main cause is related to seasonal changes in the amount of sunlight. That's why the most common form of SAD occurs during the winter when the days are shorter and there is less sunlight. Another cause is related to the changes in body temperature that occur during the winter.

The Effects of SAD

4 SAD can affect people in several ways. First of all, it can affect how you feel, or your mood. Most people with SAD get depressed for several

A patient sits in artificial light to fight SAD.

months every year. Other effects include how much you eat and sleep, and how well you deal with **stress**. For example, in the winter, some people feel tired all the time and want to be alone. They can't **concentrate** very well on work.

Treating SAD

5 A long walk in the middle of the day usually helps fight the effects of SAD. Bright lights in the home and office also help. Some people buy special lights that give off **artificial** sunlight. When spring comes, most SAD sufferers feel fine again.

SAD in the Summer

6 Some people suffer from SAD in the summer, but it is not very common. People with summer SAD may not be able to sleep or eat well. These people may feel better if they stay in air-conditioned places.

**Check
Comprehension**

A Check the topics discussed in the article.

❏ 1. which people are affected by SAD

❏ 2. how people with SAD may feel

❏ 3. the treatments for SAD

❏ 4. the causes of SAD

❏ 5. how teachers help children with SAD

❏ 6. the history of SAD

B Read these statements. If a statement is true, write *T* on the line. If it is false, write *F.*

_____ 1. Changes in the weather can affect our behavior.

_____ 2. SAD affects everyone the same way.

_____ 3. SAD affects more women than men.

_____ 4. SAD doesn't affect children.

_____ 5. The most common form of SAD occurs in the summer.

_____ 6. The lack of bright sunlight is an important cause of SAD.

**SKILL
FOR ✓
SUCCESS**

Understanding Cause and Effect
When you read, it is important to understand the **causes** (reasons) and **effects** (results) of a situation. In *Are You SAD?,* you read about several causes and effects of SAD.

C Complete the sentences with the causes and effects of SAD.

Causes of SAD include . . .

1. seasonal changes in _____.

2. changes in _____.

Effects of SAD include . . .

3. the way we _____.

4. how much we _____ and _____.

5. how well we _____.

The South Pole gets
no sunshine for
182 days per year.
The North Pole
gets no sunshine
for 176 days.
St. Petersburg,
Florida, holds the
record for the most
sunny days in a
row: 768!

A Complete each sentence with the correct word.

artificial   concentrate   depressed
mild   stress

1. Alex feels _____ in the winter. He doesn't feel like doing anything.

2. Those flowers may look real, but they are _____.

3. She has a _____ form of SAD. It doesn't affect her much.

4. Can you _____ on your homework with the TV on?

5. I don't deal with _____ very well. I feel nervous and get headaches and stomachaches.

B Ask and answer these questions with a partner.

1. What things make you feel depressed?

2. Do you like to wear natural fabrics such as cotton and wool, or artificial fabrics such as polyester?

3. Where do you go if you have to concentrate on your work or studies?

4. Does your job or school cause you stress?

5. Do you prefer foods that have a mild flavor, or a strong flavor?

✓ **Learning Synonyms and Antonyms**

C Decide if the following pairs of words are synonyms or antonyms. If they are synonyms, circle S. If they are antonyms, circle A.

1. mild   serious   S   A

2. tired   sleepy   S   A

3. intense   strong   S   A

4. depressed   sad   S   A

5. shorter   longer   S   A

6. artificial   real   S   A

✓ Learning Compound Words

D Complete each sentence with the correct compound word.

headache   mealtimes   sometimes   stomachache
sunshine   weatherman   weekends

1. My head hurts from the artificial light. I have a _____.

2. _____ I drink tea for breakfast. Other times I drink coffee.

3. I don't go to school or work on the _____.

4. The _____ said it is going to rain today.

5. People with SAD may eat more at _____ and gain weight.

6. There is less _____ in the winter.

7. I ate too much candy. Now I have a _____.

Talk It Over

Write two discussion questions based on the reading. Then exchange your questions with a partner. Discuss the answers to the questions with your partner. Finally, share your questions and answers with the class.

1. _____

2. _____

Read a Weather Forecast

A weather forecast tells what future weather is expected to be. Look at the weather forecast below. Then answer the questions that follow.

FORECAST for Baltimore, Maryland

Today's forecast—September 24

temperature: 60° F   relative humidity: 67%

cloudy   wind from the north at 9 miles per hour

5-day forecast:

Monday	**Tuesday**	**Wednesday**	**Thursday**	**Friday**
partly cloudy	sunny	cloudy	rain	thunderstorms
high 68°	high 76°	high 63°	high 78°	high 75°
low 52°	low 61°	low 49°	low 54°	low 62°

---

1. What is the current temperature for Baltimore?

   _____

2. On which days would you need an umbrella?

   _____

3. Which day is expected to have the highest temperature?

   _____

4. What is the weather supposed to be like on Friday?

   _____

5. Which day is expected to have the lowest temperature?

   _____

Tornado Chaser

Before You Read

A Discuss these questions with a partner.

1. A tornado is a very strong storm with winds that blow in a circle. Have you ever seen a tornado?
2. Have you ever seen a tornado in a movie, such as *Twister* or *The Wizard of Oz*? Describe what you saw and how it made you feel.
3. Look at the map. Tornado Alley (shaded in gray) is where most tornadoes in the United States occur. Which states does Tornado Alley include?

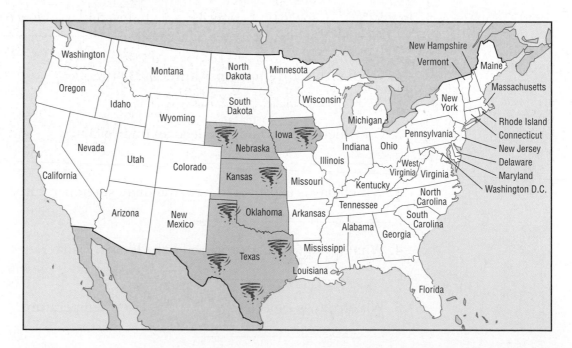

B Study these words from the article. Complete the chart. Write each word next to the correct definition.

chase   contact   damaged   powerful   precautions

1.	extremely strong
2.	things that you do to stop something bad or dangerous from happening
3.	to talk or write to
4.	to follow someone or something quickly
5.	physically harmed

Tornado Chaser

1 Every year the United States has more tornadoes than any other place on earth. Most blow through the Great Plains in an area called Tornado Alley, which includes parts of Texas, Oklahoma, Kansas, Nebraska, and Iowa. The winds from tornadoes are the most **powerful** on earth. They can blow up to 300 miles (480 kilometers) per hour. A tornado is very loud. It may sound like a train coming at you. In fact, the winds from a tornado can pick up a section of a train and throw it around.

2 Believe it or not, some people like to look for tornadoes and follow them. Chris Kridler is one of those people. Her hobby is chasing tornadoes.

3 Chris has been interested in weather since she was a kid. But she didn't begin to **chase** storms until she was an adult. Chris went on her first storm-chasing tour in 1997. This experience increased her fascination with

Tornado chaser, Chris Kridler

storms. She wanted to learn as much as she could about the weather and storm chasing. Although Chris didn't study weather in school, she learned a lot from reading information on the Internet and talking to other storm chasers.

4 According to Chris, the best time to chase storms is in the spring, when cold, dry air comes from the north and mixes with warm,

wet air from the south. This is the right condition for powerful rotating[1] thunderstorms to develop. These are the storms that can produce tornadoes.

5   Every spring, Chris drives to Tornado Alley on vacation from her job as a journalist. She fills her car with lots of equipment. She takes cameras, radios, and computers that help her find storms. Chris often meets up with friends. They get the weather forecast in the morning. Then they drive to where they think the storms will be. They choose the storm that is most likely to produce tornadoes. If they are lucky, they're in the right place to see a tornado. Sometimes they are very lucky and follow a storm that produces several tornadoes. On a single day, they may drive hundreds of miles. But if they see an amazing storm, it's all worth it.

6   Once, Chris saw four tornadoes in one day. Here's what Chris has to say about that very exciting storm chase. "My most intense storm chase was in 2004. I was with some friends as we headed toward a storm growing in Kansas. We saw a small tornado, then followed the storm east toward the town of Attica. The tornado sirens were screaming. A new tornado was forming just east of town. We headed in that direction as baseball-size hail fell around us. The tornado started to move toward us. We stopped and looked back to the west. One of the tornadoes hit the house we had just passed and ripped it apart, lifting the roof off as we watched. We called a friend

Chris watches an amazing storm.

....

and let him know, so that he could **contact** emergency workers. The storm was already producing another tornado to the east. We drove in that direction, then watched as it moved toward us. When it was time to get out of its way, a smaller tornado formed on the road directly in front of us. For a moment, we didn't know which way to go. Then it began to lose strength, and we drove east in a hurry."

7   Chris says it's not hard to stay safe on storm chases if you take **precautions** and understand which way the storm is moving. But sometimes, roads may be closed because of nearby tornadoes. This can put you in a dangerous situation. The biggest dangers are probably lightning and hail, which has seriously **damaged** her car twice. Finally, Chris says, "I do not chase storms for the excitement of it, though I do appreciate that. I chase storms so I can learn how to solve their mysteries, and so I can capture their beauty on film." ■

[1] **rotating** – going around and around

After You Read

Comprehension Check

A Read these statements. If a statement is true, write *T* on the line. If it is false, write *F.*

_____ 1. Ohio is part of Tornado Alley.

_____ 2. Chris Kridler studied weather in school.

_____ 3. Summer is the best time to study tornadoes.

_____ 4. It is Kridler's job to chase tornadoes.

_____ 5. Kridler can chase a tornado for hundreds of miles.

_____ 6. Kridler's most exciting storm chase was in 2004.

_____ 7. You can stay safe by taking precautions against a tornado.

_____ 8. The biggest danger in a tornado is thunder.

_____ 9. Kridler chases storms mainly for the excitement.

_____ 10. Kridler takes lots of pictures when she is storm chasing.

✓ **Identifying Facts and Opinions**

B Decide if each statement is a fact or an opinion. Check the correct box.

	Fact	Opinion
1. On a single day, we can drive our cars hundreds of miles.		
2. If we see a beautiful storm, it's all worth it.		
3. Our most exciting storm chase was in 2004.		
4. It was amazing to watch.		
5. On that chase, we saw four tornadoes.		
6. I think the storms of the Great Plains are beautiful and fascinating.		

Vocabulary Practice

A Complete each sentence with the correct word.

chase   contact   damaged   powerful   precautions

1. A tornado's winds are extremely _____.

2. As soon as I arrive in Paris, I am going to _____ my friend who lives there.

3. The earthquake _____ many houses and other buildings.

4. Spring is the best time to _____ tornadoes.

5. You must take _____ if you ride your bicycle at night.

B Circle the correct answer.

1. How would you <u>contact</u> your friend?
   a. forget him   b. call him

2. You might <u>damage</u> your car if you were _____.
   a. getting gas   b. in an accident

3. You should take <u>precautions</u> for a storm _____.
   a. before the storm   b. after the storm

4. A storm that has <u>powerful</u> winds is _____.
   a. weak   b. strong

5. If you <u>chase</u> your child, you _____.
   a. run after her   b. look at her

Understanding Word Parts: The Suffix -ist
The suffix *-ist* means *someone who.* For example, a *pianist* is *someone who plays the piano*.

C Complete each sentence with the correct word.

artist   biologist   journalist   physicist
scientist   typist   tourist

1. Chris Kridler studied journalism in school. Now she writes articles for her local newspaper. Chris is a _____.

2. A person who studies science is a _____.

3. A person who types is a _____.

4. Someone who studies biology is a _____.

5. Albert Einstein studied physics. He was a _____.

6. A person who travels for pleasure is a _____.

7. Picasso painted many pictures. He is my favorite _____.

Talk It Over   Discuss these questions as a class.

1. What is the worst storm you have been in? Describe it.
2. Do you think that chasing tornadoes would be fun? Why or why not?
3. Why do you think Chris finds beauty in tornadoes?

Choose Headlines   A newspaper headline usually tells the main idea of the article. Skim each article to find the main idea. Write the correct headline on the line above each article.

Disaster Brings People Together
It's Been a Long, Hot Summer
Protect Yourself from the Forces of Nature
Killer Storm Hits Coast
Bad Weather Brings Good Business

1. _____

Hurricane Babette reached the northeastern coast today and caused death and destruction everywhere. The hurricane brought heavy rain and winds of 135 miles per hour (217kph). The high winds and heavy rains combined with the force of the ocean to create extremely dangerous waves. It is not yet known how many people died or were hurt in this storm, but numbers will be very high. The damage to homes, businesses, and crops will cost billions of dollars. Now that the storm is over, the long, slow process of rebuilding will begin.

2. _____

As the temperature reaches 96 degrees for the eighth day in a row, thousands of people are escaping the heat by going to the beach. Hotels are full, and every available house has been rented. It is common to see people talking on cell phones and working on laptop computers on the beach. Meteorologists cannot predict when the heat wave will end. Whether you go to the beach or not, you should drink lots of water. Elderly and sick people should stay inside, with air-conditioning if possible. And don't forget that animals also suffer in this kind of heat. Make sure that your pets have plenty of water.

3. _____

Our area is still trying to cope with the worst flood of the century. But there are many wonderful stories of people helping other people. People from all over the world have sent food, money, and clothing to help the thousands who had to leave their homes. Many volunteers have come to help repair damaged homes and buildings. The effects of the flood will be terrible for many people, but everyone is happy to see people coming together to help others and save lives, possessions, and property.

4. _____

This winter has been one of the worst in years for many parts of the country. Many businesses suffered, but for some businesses, the cold weather and heavy storms brought big profits. For example, one chain of hardware stores sold half a million shovels this winter. This was up 75 percent from the year before. Customers also bought 50 million pounds of rock salt, which is used to melt ice. Ice scrapers were another popular item. Sales of ice scrapers in December, January, and February equaled sales of the past four years combined. Finally, sales of winter clothes were higher than ever. For example, hat sales were up 13 percent, and stores sold about 95 million pairs of gloves. One company usually sells 150,000 pairs of its most popular winter boots, but during this winter, it sold over 350,000 pairs.

5. _____

This is tornado season. If a tornado is spotted in your area, it is very important to protect yourself. Have a radio nearby, and listen to the tornado reports. A basement is the safest place to go. Try to wait under a table in the basement. If your building does not have a basement, stay on the ground floor, but lie flat under a bed or table. Do not open the windows. And stay away from them. If you are outside or in your car, try to find a low area to lie down in. Have a family plan, and teach your children these safety rules, too.

Climate and Weather

Before You Read

A Discuss these questions with a partner.

1. Do you usually listen to the weather report before you go out in the morning?
2. How accurate are the weather reports in your area?
3. What is the climate where you live?

B Study these words from the article. Complete the chart. Write each word next to the correct definition.

crops   economy   immediately

severe   transportation   typical

1.	the way that money, businesses, and products are organized in an area
2.	very bad or serious
3.	having the usual qualities of a particular group, thing, or person
4.	plants that a farmer grows
5.	now; at once
6.	the system of buses, trains, aircraft, etc., used for getting from one place to another

Taking Notes
Taking notes while you read will help you remember information.

C Use the chart below to help you take notes on the article. The main ideas are filled in. Complete the chart by filling in the details in the right-hand column.

Main Idea	Details
The main difference between weather and climate is time.	1. Weather is _what happens outdoors at a specific time and place_. 2. Climate is _____.
Severe weather is dangerous.	1. Examples of severe weather: _____, _____, _____, _____, _____. 2. Severe weather hurts _____, _____, and _____.
Several things influence the climate of a place.	1. _____ has the biggest effect. 2. _____ is important, too. 3. Other things are _____ and _____.
Climate affects us in many ways.	1. The _____ we grow 2. The _____ we wear 3. _____, _____, and _____ are also affected.
Climates around the world have changed many times throughout history.	1. 1,000 years ago, _____. 2. For millions of years, _____. 3. Scientists believe _____. 4. Global climate change is _____.

Climate and Weather

Climate and Weather

1   Weather and climate are closely related. The main difference between weather and climate is time. Weather describes what is happening outdoors at a specific place and time. Climate describes the **typical** weather of a place over many years.

Weather: A Snapshot View

2   Weather is a description of the air around us at a particular time and place. When you go outside, you notice the weather **immediately.** You can tell if it is hot or cold, raining or clear, windy or calm, cloudy or sunny, etc. You have probably noticed that the weather can change very quickly. For example, it may rain for an hour and then become sunny. A snowstorm is weather. So is rain.

Severe Weather

3   Sometimes weather can be so powerful that it is dangerous. This kind of weather is called **severe** weather. Severe weather can harm humans and the environment. Some examples of severe weather are floods, hurricanes, tornadoes, thunderstorms, and blizzards. Severe weather makes farming, industry, and **transportation** more difficult.

Climate: A Long View

4   Climate tells us what it's usually like in a place. A place that gets very

Countries close to the equator, like Nigeria, are very hot. Areas far away from the equator, like the Arctic and Antarctic, are very cold.

little rain over many years has a dry climate. A place that stays cold for most of the year has a cold climate.

What Influences Climate?

5   Meteorologists who study climate and weather say that several things influence the climate of a place. The sun has the biggest effect on climate. The sun heats the land, the oceans, and the air. An area's distance from the equator is also important. Countries close to the equator are hotter because they get more sun. For example, Nigeria is near the equator. It is one of the hottest countries in the world. Places that are farther away from the equator are colder because they do not get very much heat from the sun. The Arctic and Antarctic areas are the farthest away from the equator, so they are very cold. Other things that affect the climate of an area are mountains and oceans.

How Does Climate Affect Our Lives?

6   Climate affects our lives in many ways. For one thing, climate affects the kinds of **crops** we can and cannot grow. Therefore, it influences what we eat. Climate also affects the kinds of clothes we wear. Some places have such cold climates that people must dress warmly all the time. In hot climates, people need to wear only light clothing the whole year. Housing is affected by climate, too. For example, people who live in hot climates paint their houses white to keep the houses cooler. People who live in cold climates build houses with thick walls to keep the cold air out and the heat in. Climate can also affect the transportation and **economy** of a country.

Nomads of the Sahara Desert cover their heads for protection against sandstorms and the sun.

The Earth's Changing Climate

7   Climates around the world have changed many times throughout history. For example, a thousand years ago, places near the North and South poles were warmer than they are today. For millions of years, the earth kept changing between hot and cold, and wet and dry. As the earth warmed and cooled, plants and animals appeared and disappeared. People have had to change their way of life many times as plant and animal life changed. Some scientists believe that changes in climate have played a big part in human development.

8   Global climate change is still going on. It is affecting our planet, but it is difficult for people to recognize the effects right away because the process of climate change takes a long time.

After You Read

Comprehension Check

A Check the topics discussed in the article.

❑ 1. the difference between weather and climate

❑ 2. the typical climate in North America

❑ 3. the effects of climate on our lives

❑ 4. the factors that affect climate

❑ 5. a description of life during the coldest times on earth

B Read these statements. If a statement is true, write *T* on the line. If it is false, write *F*.

_____ 1. Climate and weather are the same thing.

_____ 2. Weather can change quickly.

_____ 3. The climate of an area always stays the same.

_____ 4. The sun has the greatest effect on climate.

_____ 5. Countries close to the equator are colder than countries farther away from the equator.

_____ 6. Climate affects human behavior in many ways.

_____ 7. The climate can affect the economic development of an area.

Vocabulary Practice

A Complete each sentence with the correct word.

crops	economy	immediately
severe	transportation	typical

> **F Y I**
>
> Antarctica is the coldest, windiest, driest, and highest continent on Earth.

1. His injuries from the accident were _____ . He almost died.

2. One of the most successful _____ in this area is corn.

3. We have a great system of _____ in our city. There are buses and trains that can take you anywhere you need to go.

4. Hot weather is _____ here in summer.

5. We need to go to the basement _____. I hear the tornado sirens.

6. The _____ of our country is getting better as more businesses are moving here.

B Ask and answer these questions with a partner.

1. What kind of transportation do you use to get to work or school?

2. What is the most important crop in your country?

3. Describe your typical day.

4. What do you do immediately after you wake up in the morning? After you get home from work or school?

5. Have you ever had a severe illness?

6. Do you think the economy of your country will get better or worse in the 21st century?

✓ **Using Superlative Adjectives**

C Use the Internet or go to the library to find the answer to each question.

1. What is the hottest place on Earth? _____

2. What is the wettest place on Earth? _____

3. What is the coldest country on Earth? _____

4. What is the driest country on Earth? _____

5. What is the windiest country on Earth? _____

Talk It Over

Discuss these questions as a class.

1. How does the climate of your area affect the kinds of clothes you wear?

2. How does climate affect the crops that can grow in your country?

3. How is the architecture of your city affected by climate?

Read a Chart

The Beaufort Scale is used to rate the speed of the wind. It was invented in 1805 by Sir Francis Beaufort of the British Navy.

Read the situations. Then scan the information in the chart on page 190 to answer each question.

1. It's a nice spring day, and you are taking your dog for walk. The birds are singing and small branches are blowing in the breeze. You see some papers blowing around on the street, and your dog runs after them and tries to catch them.

   What is the Beaufort number for the wind on this day?

   _____

2. You are walking home from the bus stop. It's raining hard, and you notice that large branches are moving on the trees. You are walking fast and trying not to get too wet. Unfortunately, it's difficult to use your umbrella because the wind is blowing.

   How many miles per hour do you think the wind is blowing?

   _____

3. You are sitting on a bench in the park, relaxing after a hard day of work. You can feel the wind on your face and smell the flowers. It's very quiet.

   How would you describe the wind? _____

4. You are walking home from school. It isn't far, but you are having a very hard time walking because the wind is blowing so hard. You can tell that a storm is coming. A twig breaks off a tree and almost hits you.

   What is the Beaufort number for the wind? _____

5. It's a beautiful winter day. The snow has just fallen, and everything looks clean and white. The smoke rises straight up from chimneys, and there is no wind. It's getting very cold, and you decide to go inside and make a fire.

   How many miles per hour do you think the wind is blowing?

   _____

Beaufort Number	Description	Miles/ Kilometers Per Hour	Effect on Land	Illustration
0	calm	less than 1	Smoke rises straight up.	
1–2	light	1–7/ 1–11	Smoke moves with air; wind can be felt on face.	
3–4	gentle, moderate	8–18/ 12–28	Leaves and small branches move; paper blows around.	
5	fresh breeze	19–24/ 29–38	Small trees move.	
6–7	strong breeze	25–38/ 39–61	Large branches move; umbrellas difficult to use; hard to walk against the wind	
8–9	gale	39–54/ 62–88	Very difficult to walk against wind; some damage to buildings and trees	
10–11	strom	55–73/ 89–117	Trees pull out of earth; lots of damage to buildings	
12–17	hurricane	74 and above/ 118 and above	Violent destruction	

Tie It All Together

Discussion

Discuss these questions in a small group.

1. Mark Twain, a famous American author, once said, "Everyone talks about the weather, but nobody does anything about it." Do you think this is a funny thing to say? Why or why not?
2. A common weather expression is, "If you don't like the weather, wait a minute and it will change." Is this true in your country?

Just for Fun

Many beliefs about the weather have been passed down from one generation to the next. Some of the following common weather expressions are true, and some are false.

Read each expression. Check the expressions you think are true. Discuss your answers as a class.

❑ 1. Bees stay close to the hive when rain is near.

❑ 2. If the groundhog sees its shadow on February 2, it becomes frightened and goes back into its hole for six more weeks. When this happens, we have six more weeks of winter.

❑ 3. Cows lie down when rain is coming.

❑ 4. If it's wet in June, it will be dry in September.

❑ 5. If birds are flying low, expect rain and wind.

❑ 6. If March comes in like a lamb, it will go out like a lion. If it comes in like a lion, it will go out like a lamb.

❑ 7. Pinecones open in dry weather and close in wet weather.

❑ 8. A heavy coat on animals or caterpillars means a long, hard winter is coming.

❑ 9. It's a sign of rain when seagulls sit on beaches.

❑ 10. When squirrels collect many nuts, expect a hard winter.

Blame the Weatherman

This video is about how some people get angry at their local weather reporters. Why do you think these people get angry?

A Study these words and phases. Then watch the video.

blame   forecast   hate mail
public   read lips   record lows
viewers   weatherman

B Read these questions and then watch the video again. Circle the correct answers. Some questions have more than one answer.

1. What season is it in the video?
   a. summer   c. winter
   b. fall   d. spring

2. Which words do you hear in the video?
   a. rain   c. heat
   b. snowstorm   d. earthquake

3. Why do viewers blame the local forecasters for the bad weather?
   a. Viewers don't like the weather.
   b. They think forecasters can change the weather.
   c. Forecasters are dishonest people.

C Discuss these questions with a partner or in a small group.

1. How do you find out about the weather forecast? TV? Radio? Internet?
2. Is it important to you to know the weather forecast? Why or why not?
3. Have you ever blamed the forecaster for making a wrong prediction about the weather?

Reader's Journal Think about the topics and ideas you have read about and discussed in this unit. Choose a topic and write about it for ten to twenty minutes. Pick a topic from the following list, or choose one of your own.

- your ideal climate
- the worst storm you have been in
- how the weather affects your mood

Vocabulary Self-Test

A Circle the correct answer.

1. Which is NOT a type of <u>transportation</u>?

   a. a boat   b. a house   c. a car

2. Which is an example of a <u>crop</u>?

   a. corn   b. computers   c. robots

3. Something that is <u>powerful</u> is _____.

   a. weak   b. clean   c. strong

4. Which is NOT an example of <u>artificial</u> light?

   a. the sun   b. a flashlight   c. a lamp

5. Which is an example of <u>severe</u> weather?

   a. a light rain   b. a blizzard   c. sunshine

B Read and answer each question. Check *Yes* or *No*.

1. When you are <u>depressed</u>, are you happy?

   ❑ yes   ❑ no

2. Is <u>mild</u> weather dangerous?

   ❑ yes   ❑ no

3. When something is perfect, is it <u>damaged</u>?

   ❑ yes   ❑ no

4. If you do something <u>immediately</u>, do you do it right now?

   ❑ yes   ❑ no

5. If hot weather is <u>typical</u> in your country all year long, is it usually cold there?

   ❑ yes   ❑ no

C Complete each sentence with the correct word.

chased   concentrate   contact

economy   precautions   stress

1. The police _____ the robber down the street.

2. Problems at work make me feel a lot of _____.

3. You should take _____ if there are tornado warnings.

4. Please _____ me when you arrive in town.

5. I can't _____ well when there is a lot of noise.

6. Our city has a good _____ and many successful businesses.

Vocabulary Self-Tests Answer Key

Unit 1
(pages 23–24)

A 1. conversation
   2. artistic
   3. suggested
   4. benefits
   5. emergency
   6. worries

B 1. advice
   2. popular
   3. athletic
   4. reservation
   5. tiny

C 1. permission
   2. appearance
   3. privacy
   4. purchase
   5. convenient

Unit 2
(pages 47–48)

A 1. fortunately
   2. temporary
   3. adventure

B 1. realize
   2. miss
   3. mistakes

C 1. borrowed
   2. frustrated
   3. cross
   4. nervous
   5. graduate

D 1. adjust
   2. flexible
   3. Occasionally
   4. suffers
   5. healthy
   6. return

Unit 3
(pages 70–71)

A 1. fascinating
   2. observed
   3. tasks
   4. pretended
   5. spot
   6. indicate

B 1. greets
   2. mood
   3. strangers
   4. circumstances
   5. proud

C 1. ingredients
   2. incredible
   3. recently
   4. poisons
   5. research
   6. mysterious

Unit 4
(pages 93–94)

A 1. talent
   2. encouraged
   3. performance
   4. achieve
   5. chance
   6. schedule

B 1. compete
   2. pay attention
   3. equipment
   4. injured
   5. active

C 1. stay in shape
   2. ceremonies
   3. participate
   4. reporter
   5. disability

Unit 5
(pages 118–119)

A 1. shy
   2. specializes
   3. verbal
   4. revolutionized
   5. memorize
   6. sense

B 1. genius
   2. curious
   3. repeats
   4. store
   5. creative
   6. logical

C 1. visual
   2. complex
   3. immigrated
   4. experiments
   5. suddenly
   6. affects

Unit 6
(pages 142–144)

1. a
2. c
3. a
4. a
5. b
6. a
7. c
8. b
9. c
10. c
11. a
12. a
13. a
14. b
15. c
16. a

Unit 7
(pages 167–168)

1. no
2. no
3. yes
4. no
5. no
6. yes
7. yes
8. yes
9. yes
10. no
11. no
12. no
13. no
14. no
15. yes
16. no
17. yes

Unit 8
(pages 193–194)

A 1. b
   2. a
   3. c
   4. a
   5. b

B 1. no
   2. no
   3. no
   4. yes
   5. no

C 1. chased
   2. stress
   3. precautions
   4. contact
   5. concentrate
   6. economy

Glossary

A

achieve (74): to succeed in doing something

active (80): doing a lot of things

adjust (40): to change in order to suit a new situation

adventure (26): an exciting experience

advertise (157): to give information about a product so people will buy it

advice (2): an opinion about what someone should do

affect (110): to produce a change in something or someone

ambitious (122): having a strong desire to be successful

annually (127): once a year

appearance (7): the way a person, animal, or thing looks to others

artificial (170): not natural; made by people

artistic (2): able to create art well

astronauts (146): people who travel and work in space

athletic (2): able to play sports well

B

benefits (16): advantages or good results

beverage (151): a drink

borrow (32): to use something that belongs to someone else and give it back later

C

ceremonies (86): important events that celebrate something

chance (74): opportunity

charities (127): organizations that give money or help to people who need it

chase (177): to follow someone or something quickly

circumstances (58): the facts or conditions that influence a situation, action, event, etc.

cloth (134): a material used to make clothes, such as cotton or wool

comfortable (134): feeling good to wear (clothes) or sit in (furniture)

compete (80): to try to win

complex (110): difficult to understand

concentrate (170): to think very carefully about something you are doing

contact (177): to talk or write to

containers (122): things you can fill, such as boxes and bottles

convenient (7): useful to you because it makes something easier or saves you time

conversations (2): talks between two or more people

creative (98): good at thinking of new ideas

crops (183): plants that a farmer grows

cross (26): to go from one side to another

curious (104): wanting to know about or learn new things

D

damaged (177): physically harmed

delicious (151): tasting very good

depressed (170): very sad

disabilities (74): illnesses or conditions that make it difficult for some people to do the things that other people do

disadvantaged (122): having problems, such as lack of money or education, that make it difficult to succeed

E

economy (183): the way that money, business, and products are organized in an area

emergencies (2): unexpected and dangerous situations

encourage (86): to give someone confidence

equipment (74): the things that you need for a particular activity

experiment (98): to try using new ideas, materials, and ways of doing things to find out how well they work

explorers (151): people who travel to unknown places to find out about them

F

fascinating (58): very interesting

fast food (157): food that is made and served quickly

flavors (127): the tastes of foods or drinks

flexible (40): able to change easily

fortunately (32): luckily

founder (122): someone who starts a business, organization, school, etc.

frustrated (32): upset because you can't get or do what you want

G

genius (104): an extremely intelligent person

give away (134): to give something to someone without asking for payment

graduated (26): got a degree

greet (58): to say hello or welcome someone

H

healthy (40): in good physical condition

I

immediately (183): now; at once

immigrated (104): came to live in a new country

incredible (50): very hard to believe

indicate (58): to show that something is probably true

ingredients (62): the things you mix together when you are making something

injured (74): hurt

J

judge (146): to decide who will be the winner of a contest

K

kids (157): children

L

logical (98): reasonable

M

manufactures (122): uses machines to make things in large numbers

market (127): to encourage people to buy something

memorize (98): to remember words, music, or other information

mild (170): not too strong or serious

missed (26): felt sad that something or someone was not present

mistake (32): something you do that is wrong

mood (58): the way you feel at a specific time

mysterious (62): strange; difficult to understand

N

natural resources (122): things such as land, plants, and oil that exist in nature and can be used by people

nervous (32): worried or frightened about something

nutritious (146): healthful

O

observed (50): watched carefully

occasionally (26): sometimes, but not often

out of this world (146): very good

overweight (157): weighing too much

P

participate (74): to be involved

pay attention (86): to watch or listen carefully

performances (86): presentations of art, music, etc., in front of others

permission (16): the act of allowing someone to do something

poison (62): something that can make you sick or kill you if you eat it, breathe it, etc.

popular (7): liked by a lot of people

powerful (177): extremely strong

precautions (177): things you do to stop something bad or dangerous from happening

prepare (146): to make or get something ready to be used

pretended (50): acted as if something was true when you knew it wasn't

privacy (16): keeping personal information secret

proud (62): pleased with something you do or have because you think it is very good

purchase (7): to buy

R

realized (32): understood something

recently (50): not very long ago

repeat (110): to say or do something again

reporters (80): people whose job is to write or tell about events in a newspaper, on TV, or on the radio

research (62): careful study, especially to find out new facts about something

reservation (7): an arrangement you make so that you have a place in a hotel, restaurant, plane, etc.

respect (151): a good opinion of or admiration for someone

responsibility (127): something that someone must do or take care of

returned (26): went back to a place

reuses (134): uses again

revolutionized (104): completely changed the way people think or do things

S

schedule (80): a plan of what you will do and when you will do it

senses (110): natural abilities such as seeing and hearing

severe (183): very bad or serious

shy (104): uncomfortable meeting and speaking with other people

snack (146): a small amount of food that you eat between meals

specializes (98): works in a specific area

spicy (151): having a strong, hot taste

spot (50): place

stay in shape (80): to keep in good health

stores (110): puts something away until it is needed

stranger (58): someone you do not know

stress (170): the feeling of being worried because of difficulties in your life

suddenly (104): quickly and without being expected

suffer (40): to experience pain or sickness

suggested (16): told someone your idea(s) about what to do

T

talent (86): the ability to do something well

tasks (50): jobs

temporary (40): happening for a short time

throw out (134): to get rid of something because you do not want or need it anymore

tiny (16): very small

transportation (183): the system of buses, trains, aircraft, etc., used for getting from one place to another

treats (151): things that you enjoy, especially to eat

typical (183): having the usual qualities of a particular group, thing, or person

U

underweight (157): weighing too little

V

verbal (98): relating to talking or words

visual (98): relating to seeing or sight

W

worry (16): to think about something that makes you feel uncomfortable or unhappy

Map of the United States

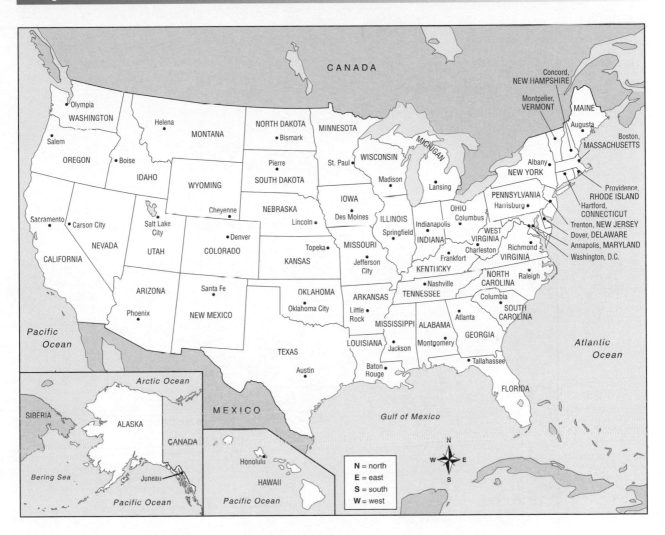

Map of the World

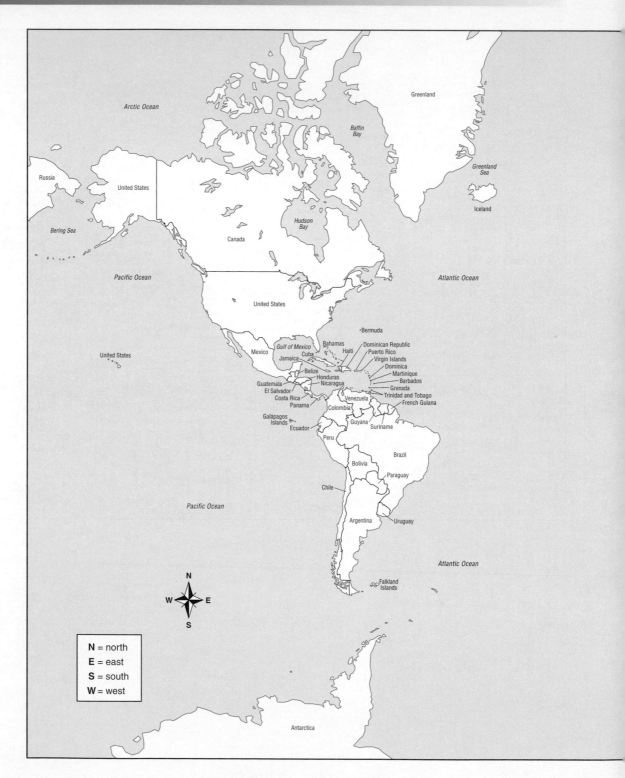

N = north
E = east
S = south
W = west

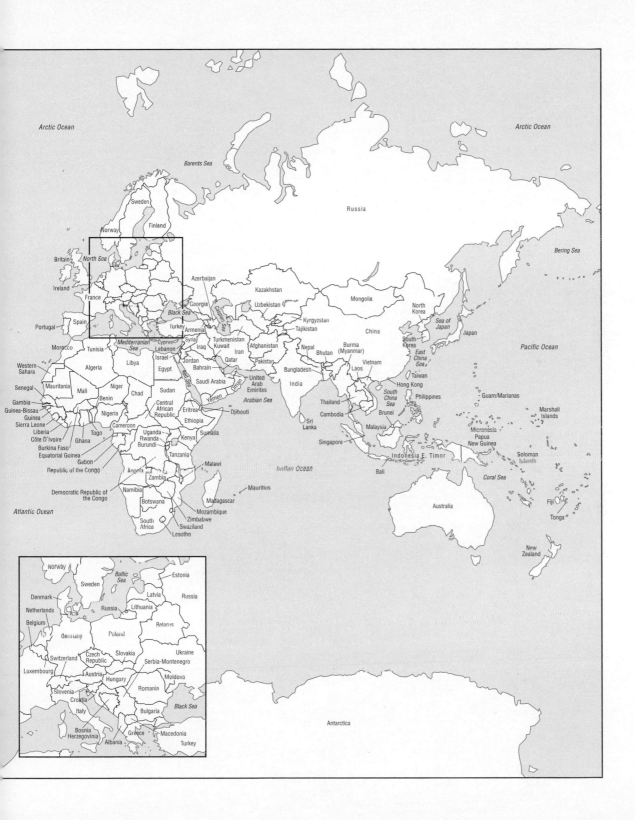

Unit 1 Tune In to Technology

_____

_____

_____

_____

_____

_____

_____

_____

Unit 2 Travel Talk

_____

_____

_____

_____

_____

_____

_____

_____

Unit 3   Animals In Our Lives

_____

_____

_____

_____

_____

_____

_____

Unit 4   Setting Goals and Facing Challenges

_____

_____

_____

_____

_____

_____

_____

_____

Unit 5   Brain Power

_____

_____

_____

_____

_____

_____

_____

Unit 6   Companies That Care

_____

_____

_____

_____

_____

_____

_____

_____

Unit 7 Food for Thought

_____

_____

_____

_____

_____

_____

_____

Unit 8 How's the Weather?

_____

_____

_____

_____

_____

_____

_____